If You Think You Can, You Can

Don Sowder

If You Think You Can, You Can

The narrative, including comments about specific events, specific individuals, specific locations, and specific timeframes are correct as I remember them. The facts are as accurate as this 86-year-old brain can comprehend and relate.

Table of Contents

Acknowledgment

I want to offer special thanks to Mary, my wife, for her loving advice, perseverance, typing, editing, and formatting of this book for publication.

Preface

Don Sowder was raised on a small farm in Southwest Virginia. The house he grew up in did not have electricity or indoor plumbing in his early years. Throughout his careers he rose above this meager beginning to hold positions of significant responsibility in the corporate world, U.S. Army, business entrepreneurship, and local government. Don had responsibility for U.S. government and military sales worldwide for Lederle Laboratories, a major pharmaceutical company. He rose to the rank of Colonel in the U.S. Army, serving as Inspector General IMA, U.S. Military Academy, West Point. After retirement, he set up a physician dinner meeting business - national in scope- headquartered in New York City. He was elected to the Board of Supervisors in Chesterfield County, bedroom community of Richmond, VA. There he served the 65,000 constituents of his Midlothian District.

During his lifetime, Don was elected by his peers to be the leader of local, state, and national organizations:

- Student body president of his high school
- Commodore, Southern Shores, NC, Boat Club
- Chairman of the Board, Virginia United Methodist Homes, Inc.
- Chairman, Association of Military Surgeons of the U.S., Sustaining Member

Don has been an active participant in community affairs everywhere he has lived. He currently lives in the mountains of Virginia near Roanoke.

Early Years

Daaaaa-nald – GET UP! It was my dad calling from outside the house on a typically cold winter day. He had already fed and watered the chickens, and it was now my turn to help him with the pigs and cows in the predawn hours before I had to get ready for school.

"Is this call for real? Is it really that time of day, or am I just dreaming?" I'm dreaming as I snuggle down under several quilts, the only source of comfort in that cold upstairs bedroom with no heat, while being aware of cold drafts coming around the window that was frosted on the inside. "Daaaaa-nald! I said it's time to get up!!!" Immediately, alertness overtook me as I quickly wiggled from under the covers and emerged into the shivering coldness of the dark room with no electrical lighting. I surely did not want to experience my Daddy's wrath over falling back to sleep. I quickly relieved myself in the small chamber pot that was under the bed and ran downstairs to the warmth of the kitchen/sitting room. This room was heated by a wood-burning cook stove, where my mother was already preparing breakfast and lunches for the day.

Mama already had my clothes laid out so I could dress in the warmth rather than in the coldness of my upstairs bedroom. I got dressed quickly and headed off to meet Dad at the barn. The path that led down the hill about 100 yards to the barn was easy to follow in the dark, as I had done it many times before. The light from Daddy's lantern gave good directional signals if I veered from the path.

I started my chores at the barn, which were routine – milk two or three cows, get grain or other food from the grainery to feed the hogs, cows, and growing calves, as well as horses. As usual, I climbed into the loft to throw down enough hay to provide a day's rations for the animals. I actually enjoyed milking because the warmth of the cows' udders provided warmth to my cold hands. In fact, I discovered an especially warm place between the cow's udder and leg. I used this option frequently to warm my hands.

After the barn chores were done, I headed back to the house for a nice hot breakfast. Breakfast consisted of eggs, sausage, biscuits, and often white gravy. Mama always saw to it that my dad, Joyce Ann (my older sister), and I got a good start for the day with a hot breakfast – all prepared on that wood-burning cook stove.

By now it was 7:00 a.m., after two hours of farm chores, and time to leave for school. I headed to the school bus which was parked in our driveway at the foot of our hill. Daddy was the school bus driver, so that made catching the bus pretty easy. I enjoyed the school bus ride of about one and a half hours, as this was a time to talk with my friends. The ride home was a bit less enjoyable, as I dreaded to face another one of my chores - cleaning up the school bus. This was to be followed with a repeat of all my barn chores, which occurred twice every day. Surprise!!! Farm life is 24/7 with no weekends or holidays.

Callaway Elementary School

Nestled in the foothills of The Blue Ridge Mountains, near the entrance to The Blue Ridge Parkway, is the little hamlet of Callaway, VA. Callaway is a typical, small, mountain village with a general store, a make-shift garage, two small churches, and a few small houses anchored by the impressive Barnhart and Robertson residences, which were a bit out of place given the simplicity of the neighborhood. The village is divided by the lazy Blackwater River, which becomes a raging mass of uncontrollable water after big mountain rains. All the mountain rains seem to converge in this little village with severe flooding.

It is in this setting that the Callaway Elementary School educates kids of mountaineers, bootleggers, farmers, and factory workers. E.M. Simpson, the principal, is in complete control of the operation. Mr. Simpson is a strict, old-school disciplinarian, but also displays compassion for the students and community, as well. Mr. Simpson's medical clinic is held daily prior to classes getting underway. While his medical training is limited or questionable at best, nevertheless, he is the only medical contact that many kids and some community residents ever have. Daily he treats scratches, bruises, dog bites, and pain with his magical potions and salves. One of his specialties is removing warts, which I can confirm with the scar on top of my middle finger, but alas, the wart is gone!

After medical clinic is over, the dreaded disciplinary period is a daily event. Behavioral problems that the teacher cannot handle are referred to Mr. Simpson. For most of us kids, the threat of that trip to Mr. Simpson's office is more than adequate to keep us in line. Mr. Simpson's discipline varies from a tongue-lashing to being restricted to his office during recess to an outright whipping with a paddleboard or belt.

Miss Stone, my third-grade teacher was also a pretty good disciplinarian in her own right. She left the classroom frequently to take a smoke break. Upon departing the classroom, she threatened all of us with the typical punishment if we talked or became too loud. As would be expected of third graders, we enjoyed the opportunity to talk, laugh, and be generally noisy. And, yes, upon Miss Stone's return we all got the typical punishment - we held up our hands, palm up, while she spanked them with a wooden ruler - no damage to the hands, but WOW! Did it ever sting!

I remember well my first day at Callaway Elementary School. Mama had put Joyce Ann, my sister who is three years senior to me, in charge of getting me to the right room. After a long summer with limited opportunity to see her friends, her focus was on getting back together with them. Joyce Ann did not need her little brother hanging around to embarrass her. Accordingly, she pointed out my first-grade teacher to me and told me to stay with her so that I would end up in the right room. Dutifully, I followed my teacher everywhere she went, of course keeping my distance. Among her travels was a visit to the lady's room; unaware to her, with me in tow. Upon recognizing me, she motherly asked me to wait outside, which I did.

Another memorable event that involved Joyce Ann was again her failure to follow her mama's instructions to protect her little brother. While not evident 80+ years later, I had a full and heavy head of hair. Right in the middle of my forehead was a major 'cowlick' which stood straight up; to say that it was unruly was no doubt the understatement of the year. Mama's efforts to make the best of this unmanageable condition consisted of pasting the 'cowlick' down with some gooey substance and pinning it down with bobby pins. She instructed Joyce Ann to remove the bobby pins before anyone else got on the bus to save me from embarrassment. As you probably guessed, Joyce Ann failed to remove the bobby pins, and needless to say, I was the object of some ridicule when older boys recognized my unusual hairstyle. Looking back, I've had a lot of challenges in repairing my self-esteem. Overall, my experience in

Callaway school was very pleasant and productive. It was there that I met my good friend, H.N. Barnhart, as well as my first childhood girlfriend, Betsy Naff. I was respected by the teachers, if not a bit spoiled, as they all knew my parents and interacted with them in the community. They all did their very best to provide a good foundation for our future education and life choices.

Growing up and being educated in a small school in a close-knit, country neighborhood had its advantages. As kids we all knew that if we were disciplined at school for misbehavior, our parents would be informed. Of course, that meant we received a second course of discipline at home. For the most part, I was a pretty good kid. The "facts are", I didn't have much choice! As I said, the teachers and the principal knew my parents, and when I left school, I rode on the bus where my Daddy was the driver and disciplinarian.

Piedmont Presbyterian Church

One of the two churches in the village of Callaway was Piedmont Presbyterian Church (PPC), an institution that helped shape my growing up years. From early childhood, Mama and Daddy saw to it that we were in church every Sunday and frequently some nights during the week. Daddy was not a very religious man, or if he was, he never talked about it. Mama was the religious one that drove our connection to PPC. She was an avid Bible reader and career Sunday School teacher.

In addition to Sunday activities, PPC is the hub of social activities in the community for members and their children. My memories of PPC are mostly positive. My first Sunday School teacher was Miss Bernice Jamison, an 'old maid' who was handicapped physically as well as having a severe speech impediment. Her claim to fame was her love for people, in particular children. Despite her handicaps, she taught me and my classmates about Jesus by reading Bible stories with her broken English. In Sunday School class as children, we played, we sang songs, and we learned to respect Miss Bernice as our teacher and our friend. The other teacher I remember was Mr. Joe Jamison, who was a saint. He was my teacher when I was about 9-12 years old. He had to be a saint in order to put up with the rowdy kids in his class. I had no interest in what he was trying to teach despite his efforts to make the class interesting; but he did teach me by example. We often went on excursions to The Blue Ridge Parkway, picnics, parties at his house, and other fun outings. It was during these events that I began to admire him as a teacher, model human-being, and example to follow.

During childhood and as a young adult, I was active at PPC. We had several ministers. For the most part, they were fundamentalist preachers. They kept me scared most of the time! It seemed to me that everything I did or even thought about had me headed on a straight path to hell. Fortunately, as I matured into my teens, I began to see my beliefs in a more positive way. It was at PPC that I had the first opportunity to practice my vocal abilities through singing. I sang in duets, trios, and quartets with Joyce Ann and friends; yup, still reluctant to attempt a solo. Despite my timidity as a singer in my early years, the PPC experience developed in me an appreciation of singing. Throughout most of my life I have been involved in church choirs and other musical ventures. I have organized and performed with country and bluegrass groups, and, yes, have even sung as a soloist.

PPC has had a significant impact on my upbringing, and as years have gone by, I realize much has stayed with me. I am most thankful that Mama and Daddy, in particular Mama, made church experience a meaningful part of my life. PPC established a foundation for me that has lasted a lifetime. While there have been periods of less-than-dedicated involvement with a church, as I have matured, the church and my faith in God have become a routine and necessary part of my lifestyle.

Franklin County High School

As a rural community, Franklin County for many years had a series of elementary schools and small high schools located in populated settlements to educate its youth. A typical high school had from 10-20 students. As a farming and factory worker county, many students dropped out of school after the seventh grade or one to two years of high school. Education resources and teachers were challenged because of the small number of students.

In the early 1950's, a consolidated high school designed to accommodate all county students was built and opened. This represented a major change for education and a dramatic improvement for county high school students. The consolidation of resources into a single state-of-the-art facility made it possible for students to receive the best in specialized teachers, laboratory facilities, arts, etc. Timing was great for me to be part of this new experiment. I started attending Franklin County High School as a Junior in 1953. It proved to be the first major change in my perspective on life and its opportunities. For me, it was the opening of a new world. All at once, I was exposed to students whose parents were merchants, bankers, physicians, and small business entrepreneurs, as compared to mostly farm families with whom I spent my early years growing up.

High school was an exciting and life-changing time for me. I looked forward each day to the challenge and excitement of this new venture. School buses brought students from all areas of the county to the town of Rocky Mount, site of Franklin County High School. While the bus was my primary source of transportation, on many days I was able to carpool with my friends, H.N.,

Betsy, Velma Jo, and sometimes Johnny. On most days, at least one of them had access to a car. On rare occasions, I was able to work a deal with Dad to use the family car. To say the least, it was quite a status symbol to arrive at school in a car rather than the school bus. Of course, an extra benefit of the car was the ability to stop off at the steakhouse (high school hangout) after school. This after-school option made it possible for me to get to know some of the town kids. The high school jocks and cheerleaders were all part of our after-school gatherings. Among all the new students I met, one stood out well above the others. As luck would have it, on a day that I was fortunate enough to have Dad's car, I was able to make my first move. Beverly, that special person who stood out above the rest, had an embarrassing accident that provided me the opening. She spilled a carton of chocolate milk in her skirt, which saturated the entire front. She was a mess! In my timid, but princely manner, I offered to take her home to change. She lived in town just a few blocks from the school. She graciously accepted my offer. This was the start of a fifty-year love life and relationship that lasted until her untimely death from pancreatic cancer. We bonded immediately after the chocolate milk experience and dated through high school. She was one year ahead of me in school, and when she left Rocky Mount for Mary Washington College, we had a brief period of reevaluation. We shortly thereafter reunited, and the rest is history. During our dating at FCHS, Beverly encouraged me to run for student body president. She said, "You'd be a great choice, and I'll be your campaign manager." My primary competition, Wayne Bennett, was a high school jock, a great student, teacher's pet, and to complicate matters with families – he was Beverly's next-door neighbor.

I needed some encouragement and guidance. I remember to this day – after completing my farm chores, and after the stars were out, I went outside, looked up into the heavens, and uttered a simple, but sincere prayer. I asked the Lord for guidance. I remember so well that inaudible yet real voice that said, "If you think you can, you can."

I did agree to run, and Beverly organized a great campaign complete with lots of supporters. I won the election and served as student body president, the first leadership role that I had experienced. That experience changed my life and has been a model for many leadership roles in my civilian and military careers. I have lived my life with the thought – "If you think you can, you can."

Virginia National Guard

Until the mid-50's, the town of Rocky Mount had never had a National Guard unit. The word got around that a unit was being formed. The word was that you would be provided with free U.S. Army uniforms and equipment. In addition, you would be paid upwards of $3.00/drill. To seal the deal, during the summer you would travel to exotic places for summer camp. This excitement caught my attention. I could sure use the $3.00, and I always liked the look of soldiers. Travel beyond Roanoke, VA (which had been my normal idea of travel) seemed very exciting indeed. After a brief conversation with an old World War II sergeant, I joined up. The armory had not yet been built, so our weekly drills were in the Coca-Cola building, the American Legion building, or any other available, vacant location. All members of the unit were wet-behind-the-ears high school kids looking for adventure.

In the early days of the unit's formation, we were told that the battalion commander, a lieutenant colonel, would be coming to town for a visit. He would lead a huge parade of the unit around town. We were conditioned to believe that he was God in uniform. As an incentive to look sharp, we were told that the sharpest soldier in the unit would drive the lieutenant colonel's jeep in a parade around town. I decided right then that person would be me. I enlisted my mother's help with my khakis; she had so much starch in them that when they were pressed, they would stand alone. I worked on my boots and brass for weeks; I worked so hard on spit-shining my boots that I just about ran out of spit. The brass was shined so much that it probably reduced the size of the brass insignia. Nevertheless, on the morning of the parade and the intense inspection, the company commander announced "Private Sowder, you will be the battalion commander's driver in the parade." Was I ever proud! And yes, that old saying came back to me: "If you think you can, you can."

Finally, the summer rolled around, and it was time for our exotic place for summer camp to be revealed; it was Bethany Beach, Delaware. Of course, no one had ever heard of Bethany Beach, Delaware. We departed Rocky Mount on a motor march in military convoy for an unknown location at about 4:15 a.m. At about 11:00 p.m., we discovered we were in Norfolk, VA, near the entrance to the Chesapeake Bay. At that time, the eighteen-mile crossing was by ferry, as the bridge-tunnel had not been built. The night air was foggy with a persistent mist. The convoy had stopped just short of the bay for a rest period and smoke break.

Prior to the truck engines starting for the continuation of our trip, the sergeant came by our truck of tired young mountaineers and announced, "Fellows, we have had a change of orders; we are going overseas." That got our attention and started a series of speculations. We all concluded that the sergeant was just pulling our legs. Our mind was abruptly changed as we could see a huge ocean-going vessel, and the trucks in front were loading on the vessel. I had never seen a ferry and had never seen a large body of water the size of the ocean. The largest body of water I had ever seen was Blackwater River, which is about 30-feet across. Oh my! The sergeant was telling the truth – we are going overseas, and we may never see our parents or family again. The mind of a seventeen-year-old can be misguided, particularly in a strange setting. Being in the middle of the Chesapeake Bay, which I thought was the ocean (at midnight on a rainy night), surely played tricks on this kid who grew up in the mountains; after all, I was not sure I'd told my mother I'd be gone for two weeks!! Now I'm going overseas! How relieved I was to see land on the far side of the Chesapeake Bay in the morning hours.

Upon debarkation, we proceeded to Bethany Beach, DE, which would be our encampment for the next two weeks. As an anti-aircraft artillery battery, we spent our days shooting our big guns at sleeves that were towed by airplanes down the beach. These sleeves were about 200 yards behind the planes. If the pilots of the tow plane had any idea just how green we were at our jobs, they would have been petrified.

We worked diligently each day for the evening excitement that was to come in Ocean City, Maryland. WOW!!! How could you ever describe to a young mountaineer boy who had hardly been 30 miles from home what to expect at a place like Ocean City, MD. It's an understatement to say that it appropriately fit the description of exotic. I quickly concluded that if this is what the army is about, I'm in it for the long haul. As it turned out, I did serve for a total of 33 years between active-duty Army, Virginia National Guard, and U.S. Army

Reserve. The bulk of my Virginia National Guard service occurred after a stint in the active Army. Much of the Guard service was served in the Norfolk, VA, area. During this time, I served as Aide-de-Camp to the commanding general of the 29th Infantry Division. The famous 29th was one of the key divisions in the D-Day landing at Normandy and the senior command of the Bedford Boys, who lost their lives in the invasion. The town of Bedford, VA, lost more soldiers per capita in this invasion than any other community in America. In addition to the Aide duties, I also served as a platoon leader, executive officer, and headquarters battery commander in the first battalion of the 111th field artillery. Both the 29th division and the 111th field artillery have proud histories being among the lead elements of the D-Day invasion in World War II.

The highlight of my experience in the 111th was winning the annual direct fire shoot. My battery (headquarters battery) is the unit which takes care of administration and logistics for the battalion. This includes support functions such as personnel management, finance, medical, communications, food service, and supplies. My troops were not experts in operation of the big Howitzers (105mm artillery pieces). This is the role of the firing batteries. Artillery, by nature, has its impact by delivering indirect fire. However, as a defensive measure, it can be used as a direct fire weapon. To add some excitement to the direct fire shoot, I asked the battalion commander if my headquarters battery could participate. With rolling eyes and a chuckle, he agreed. During the weeks leading up to the event, I and my men had to endure ridicule from the firing battery personnel. To counteract this humiliation, I was able to motivate my men to believe we could possibly win. Again, that old saying kicked in: "If you think you can, you can." We had cooks, medics, personnel specialists, and supply clerks training hard on our borrowed Howitzers during the weeks leading up to the big event. The firing battery personnel, already experts on the operation of the Howitzer, saw additional training as just going through the motions. On the big day of the direct shoot, to the surprise of the battalion commander and the three firing battery commanders, the winning battery was my headquarters battery. What a celebration it was for this unlikely win!

College Days

It was a foregone conclusion that I would attend VPI for my higher education. Why? It's the only university I considered. Callaway, VA, is a farming community, largely dairy farmers. For the young farm boys who did not want a career in farming, the way out was to go to VPI, get a degree in dairy science (manufacturing and technology), and ultimately get a job with Sealtest Foods or some other dairy manufacturing company. Several of my cousins and an uncle whom I looked up to took that route. At the time, I did not explore other options.

Arriving at VPI (now VA Tech) and being a 'rat' in the Corps of Cadets was a real wakeup call. After having been one of the leaders and a part of the 'in' gang at Franklin County High School, becoming the lowest thing on the planet as a 'rat' in the Corps got my attention in a hurry. "Square that corner, Rat!"; "Brace, Rat!!"; "Your shirt tuck stinks, Rat!"; "I can't see my face in your shoes, Rat!"; "You call that shining your brass, Rat??" The hazing I endured that first year from upper classmen was probably the worst year I ever experienced in my life. As I look back, it had taught me that I could endure almost anything that the world could throw at me in the future. "If you think you can, you can." While the Corps of Cadets still has the first year 'rat' system, the focus is now on a gentler way to teach leadership and discipline. During my sophomore year, I took advantage of the opportunity to make the incoming 'rats' feel like the scum of the earth as I had experienced; but I also began to realize that regardless of class, I was a part of a brotherhood that would last for a lifetime. Despite the first year's challenges, the goal over four years is to develop leaders of character to serve the country in uniform or as leaders in the civilian world. The Corps taught me leadership skills, endurance, time management, and moral principles that have helped me live a successful life in a non-forgiving and complex world. To this day, I attribute my Corps experience as the most significant takeaway from VPI in terms of living a productive life.

During the years I attended VPI, every student was a member of the Corps of Cadets; the only exceptions were veterans going to school on the GI Bill and a very few girls. Girls were not required, nor in fact allowed, to be members of the Corps; most girls came to VPI to study Home Economics. All girls at VPI lived in Hillcrest Hall, which was affectionately referred to as the "skirt barn."

All our classroom activities revolved around the Corps. The entire Corps had early morning Reveille - formation for inspection prior to marching to Owen Hall for breakfast as a unit. After the day's classes, drills and other activities were over, the entire Corps formed again for retreat ceremonies and marching to dinner.

My educational focus was on the manufacture of dairy products (such as various types of cheeses, milk products, ice cream, sour cream, etc.) and the laboratory procedures to ensure proper testing. Much of my classroom activity was in the chemistry, biology, and bacteriology departments.

As it was necessary for me to work to pay for college expenses, I had a variety of jobs during my stay at VPI; the first was to collect milk samples from all the facilities that the VPI creamery supplied. I would acquire samples, take them back to the lab, and perform a standard plate count to determine bacterial content. This was done by inoculating a petri dish that had a special agar previously prepared for a food source. I incubated the petri dishes for 24 hours and then counted the bacteria microscopically. While the total bacterial count was frequently high, E. Coli contamination was a special red flag. This indicated the less-than-desirable processing and handling of milk products. My reports of high E. Coli counts set off inspections at all levels from the farm to daily processing to delivery.

Another job I had was as a waiter at the Faculty Center. As university standards go, the Faculty Center was a relatively high-end restaurant where many faculty members and college administrators had lunch. Two memories of that experience stand out in my mind. First, I learned that college faculty members have a record of being the poorest tippers of all diners. A tip of $.10 was luxury from this group. Secondly, it's the place where I got the nickname "shakes" from my fellow waiters. When serving a large table, we often had a tray of eight to ten meals, which we carried over our head with one hand. A major mishap could occur if your tray became off-balanced. Supposedly, some of my guests were a bit uneasy when I had a large tray of meals over their heads; thus, the name "shakes" caught on and followed me for several years. One of the advantages of this job was being able to have a super, free lunch. My final job while at VPI was working at the Sealtest condensery in Christiansburg; more about that later.

As I was dating Beverly, my high school girlfriend, during this time I made trips to Rocky Mount as often as possible. That was a challenge, as I did not have a car. If I was lucky, I was able to catch a ride with another student, but I was often left to the mercy of hitchhiking. Hitchhiking was very common in those days, and if you were in your cadet uniform, chances for a pickup were very good. Thankfully with the help of a loan from my father, eventually I was able to obtain a decent used car in my junior year. The justification for the car was my need to drive about ten miles to Christiansburg for my new job.

Before the luxury of having my own car, life was hectic. Between keeping up with schoolwork, Corp, job, and trips to Rocky Mount on weekends to see Beverly, the pace was getting to me. With the wisdom of two 19-year-olds in love, Beverly and I started discussing marriage as a solution to the problem. Whether logical or illogical, the plan was rapidly taking shape. At some point, we got up the courage to share our plan with our parents. While both sets of parents displayed a fair amount of skepticism, they became supportive. More appropriately it would be better to say, they accepted the inevitable. So, on a November night in 1957, we had a wedding that was the talk of the town at the Rocky Mount United Methodist Church.

Our honeymoon was in Washington, DC, with our first night at the Natural Bridge Hotel. We arrived at about 2:00 a.m. and signed in with Beverly still wearing her hat. I nervously signed the registration book as Mr. and Mrs.

R. D. Sowder, and immediately recognized that it was incorrect. I announced to the attendant, "This is my Daddy's name!" - hard to determine whether the attendant's look of amusement or Beverly's look of embarrassment was most notable. We continued to Washington, DC, the next day and stayed at the first Marriott Hotel ever built. It was located near Reagan National Airport and has been removed for many years for what is now Pentagon City commercial area. We were lucky to even arrive at the hotel considering neither of us knew anything about the Washington area. Driving toward the city I could see the Marriott lights off to the right in the distance, so I told Beverly to keep the Marriott in sight so we would not miss the turn-off. I could tell that the Marriott was passing us by on the right as we were headed across the 14th Street Bridge in Washington, DC. Whooops! Missed the turn-off. We turned around, headed back, and once again pictured the Marriott off to the right in the distance. I reiterated to Beverly to carefully look for the exit to the Marriott. We're driving straight ahead, and guess what - the Marriott is passing us by again! I said, "Beverly, you missed the turn," so we turned around and repeated our approach for the third time - this time, determined to 'catch' the exit. Coming from Rocky Mount, VA, we were accustomed to turning off to the right for destinations to the right. Welcome to the big city!! We had to go to the left and under the highway to get to the Marriott, but this time we made it. Overall, we had a great three-day honeymoon and even were able to laugh at our blunders as newlyweds.

After the honeymoon, Beverly returned to Rocky Mount, where she was living with her parents. She had completed a year at Mary Washington College and was now a day student at National Business College in Roanoke, VA. I returned to VPI in Blacksburg and to my hectic routine. This arrangement would have to last until I could figure out a way for us to live together in Blacksburg. In the meantime, I was in Rocky Mount from Friday evening to Sunday evening. We spent the weekends with Beverly's parents.

Fortunately for me, my uncle and mentor, Carl Bussey, lived in Blacksburg. He was the Zone Manager of Sealtest Foods, which included the dairy manufacturing plant in Christiansburg. Through his benevolence, I was able to get a job which made it possible for me to complete my schoolwork with a reduced academic load during the school day and work at the dairy manufacturing plant at night. I was able to work from 5:00 p.m. to 11:00 p.m. every other day, including Saturdays, Sundays, and holidays. The money from that job, plus a monthly-advanced ROTC check, made it possible for me to rent one of four apartments that were located above a drywall warehouse on Giles Road in Blacksburg. Whoooo! At last, we could live together as a couple no matter how meager our lifestyle. In fact, to supplement our skimpy resources, Beverly planned to work in Blacksburg. I don't know how, but nature intervened, and she informed me that she was pregnant. So much for 20-year-old wisdom!! I now had an additional year of college to complete, a pregnant wife who was unable to work, and soon-to-be new baby to support on my meager resources.

Oh well, all the married students living in town had similar circumstances, and we became very good friends with many other young, married student couples: T.O. and Frances Williams, Phil and Nancy Long, Charlie and Ann Weaver, Bill and Cathy White, George and Martha Hennan, among others. Many of these couples became lifelong friends. Looking back, those days (despite hardships, long hours, limited resources) were some of the best days of my life.

One of my great memories is flying with George. George was a brand-new second lieutenant in the Air Force who had just completed flight school and was assigned to VPI as an ROTC instructor. George and Martha were one of the four couples who lived on our floor in the apartment. While George was an Air Force officer and I was an Air Force ROTC Cadet, there was a world of difference in our status. Yet, as a senior cadet soon to be commissioned as a second lieutenant, I had much in common with George and we soon became friends and shared the love of flying. As circumstances would have it, I was later commissioned into the U.S. Army.

George had total access to use of the Air Force plane that was stationed at the Blacksburg Airport. It was a Piper L-20, single-engine aircraft, which we loved to fly. I was invited to fly with him when I could work it into my hectic schedule. He gave me a lot of "stick" time flying, and I learned a lot from him about the basics of flying. I loved every minute of this experience, and in particular that I was treated as an equal and friend. I later took flying lessons on my own and flew for a brief period as a civilian aviator in the Norfolk area. While my initial goal in the Corp was to become an Air Force pilot, I switched from Air Force ROTC to Army ROTC at the start of my junior year. My eyesight for Air Force pilot requirements was marginal, so I became an Army officer instead.

The unplanned-for-arrival of Reid, my oldest son, presented an equal measure of challenges, happiness, and growing up fast. We had lots of help and support from parents, siblings, other married students, and friends, but the major credit goes to Beverly. I remember well arriving home from my work at the Sealtest plant at 11:30 p.m. after having attended classes during the day and working from 5:00 p.m. to 11:00 p.m. I was a tired camper, but Beverly had been cooped up from early morning until 11:30 p.m. with a baby who at the time did much more crying than laughing. Needless to say, she was a tired camper, as well. With some luck, we each got a small amount of sleep before the routine started again the next day. We each learned early on that it is possible to do things that we never imagined. "If you think you can, you can."

During the early years of my college experience, I also had some memorable summers. VPI Dairy Science Department had a strong relationship with Sealtest Foods, largely due to Uncle Carl Bussey, who was a zone VP of Sealtest. A summer internship had been established with Sealtest Foods in Norfolk, VA, for a promising student in Dairy Technology. Thankfully, because of Uncle Carl's influence at Sealtest and VPI, I was selected to fill the position after one full year of studies in Dairy Technology. Needless to say, I was thrilled at the thought of spending an exciting summer in Norfolk near the excitement offered by the beach and the big city. As I made my way to Norfolk from Rocky Mount (an eight-hour drive with no interstates), I had grandiose thoughts about my summer at Sealtest. How big would my office be? What would my secretary look like? How many people would I supervise? After all, I was a college man, right?!!! When I got to the outskirts of Norfolk, I asked for directions to the Sealtest plant from the first person I saw. The response – "I've never heard of Sealtest" – my first introduction to the real world. After finding the plant across the railroad tracks on the wrong side of town and discovering a once white building that was grayed by the effect of smoke from passing trains, reality was starting to come into focus. Oh well, I would only have to look at the building until I was ushered to my spacious, walnut-paneled office by my secretary…. after all, I'm a college man, right?!!!

After I parked my car, I spotted a man moving milk cans on the shipping dock, so I eagerly introduced myself - "Hi, I am Don Sowder!!" He reluctantly acknowledged my presence with "Yes?" - Wow!! Someone forgot to notify the employees that a new college man would be arriving. After I explained my status, he announced that he would try to locate my supervisor. "Supervisor???" – I thought **I** would be the supervisor – "After all, I **am** a college man!" Eventually, a middle-aged man dressed in what were once white coveralls now covered with chocolate ice cream stains showed up. Tom was the ice cream department supervisor who informed me that my first task would be straining strawberries. In a nutshell, that meant dumping five-gallon cans of strawberries into a separator that put berries in one vat and juice in another: an essential step in making strawberry ice cream. Well, so much for the life of a new college man at Sealtest. No big office, no secretary, no one to supervise; instead, a basic introduction to humility and the real world of Sealtest.

All in all, I enjoyed two summer internships at Sealtest in Norfolk. Although many of the tasks were menial, it helped me learn from the ground floor up the many aspects of manufacturing dairy products. As I gained competence, I was assigned the responsibility of starting the pasteurizing and homogenizing equipment for the day's run of bottled milk. I was required to come in at 2:00 a.m. to start the operation, which at times was challenging after a fun time the night before. Essentially, the job was to run raw milk from holding tanks into finished product tanks of pasteurized-homogenized milk. An essential requirement was to shift the milk flow from a full tank to an empty tank at the appropriate time; boring, to say the least, particularly for a sleep-deprived boy in the early morning hours. More than once, I was awakened by a stream of milk in my sleepy face from a full tank due to my neglect in changing the valve at the appropriate time. All in all, my two summers of internship were a great learning experience. Most importantly, I was able to spend time at the beach - a special treat for a mountain farm boy. To top it all off, it was the most money I had ever made; enough to make a big dent in the next years' college expenses.

After Graduation

As a graduate of VPI and the VA Tech Corps of Cadets, I was commissioned a Second Lieutenant in the U.S. Army, Field Artillery branch. Soon after graduation I received orders for Fort Sill, OK, where I completed the Field Artillery Officers Basic Course. This was the start of a 33-year career in the Army, much of which was inactive duty in the Virginia National Guard, U.S. Army Reserve, and active-duty U.S. Army IMA positions.

My long military career was due to my love of the military, options to develop and expand my leadership skills, and as you will learn later, it blended with my civilian career. In my civilian job I had responsibility for all sales to military facilities in the USA, as well as all military units assigned to overseas locations and ships at sea. This was a natural tie-in which benefited my success, both as a pharmaceutical industry executive and as a senior military officer. This mutually supportive relationship gave me access to many high-level military leaders at the Department of Defense (DOD) level, which benefited my pharmaceutical employer. It also provided me with experiences that enhanced my promotional opportunities in the Army. My duty stations, some of which were short-term active-duty assignments, included Fort Sill, OK, Fort Knox, KY, Fort Meade, MD, Fort Belvoir, VA, Fort Polk, LA, and the U.S. Military Academy at West Point, NY. My overseas civilian work included administrative orders in Germany, England, and Italy. Notable military assignments included Battery and Battalion command positions, Director NCO Academy, Command and General Staff College instructor, Military Academy Field Admissions Officer, and Inspector General U.S. Military Academy.

My military and civilian careers were mutually supportive and gave me many opportunities to use leadership skills. I never felt like I was going to work. Both careers provided exciting opportunities every day.

Life As a Sales Representative

After my active-duty stint in the Army, it was only natural for me to start my first job in the dairy industry. Off to Norfolk, VA! I went with Beverly and young son, Reid, where I would become a sales representative for Sealtest Foods. It was a great place to experience the real world and interact with my peers and customers as well. It was my first realization on the job that all salespeople do not have the same degree of enthusiasm for their work. As in most industries, a small percentage of the work force produces the major share of the results.

My daily routine on a typical day included calling on competitive accounts to secure their business, as well as calling on current customers to increase product usage by employing good merchandising techniques. In the '60's, most ice cream was sold in drug stores, via milk shakes, sodas, sundaes, etc. at the soda fountain. My job was to convert drug stores and grocery stores who sold Pet, Meadow Gold, Swift, or other brands of ice creams or dairy products to Sealtest. In addition to converting accounts to Sealtest, I also sold soda fountain and ice cream and milk display cases. At the risk of bragging, which I am, I was a great salesman. I once sold a dairy and food display case to a small neighborhood grocery store that was too large to be installed through the store entrance door; the front of the store had to be removed and replaced! Yet, the store owner was happy with his purchase. I enjoyed the work, worked hard, and often led my peers in frequent sales contests.

In my selling efforts to drug stores, I developed a friendship with an Upjohn drug representative, Jim Anderson. This led to my exploration of the drug industry and eventually being hired by Lederle Laboratories. This was the start of 30+ years with Lederle, in addition to another 20 years of various consulting jobs. I also started a drug symposium business in New York City from scratch. I would learn that a change from the dairy industry to the pharmaceutical industry is a remarkable and unlikely shift. But! "If you think you can, you can."

The life of a drug rep in the late '60's was exciting and considerably different than that of a drug rep today. Computers, the Internet, smart phones, GPS, and other conveniences we take for granted were non-existent or in their infancy. The drug rep was the primary source of information for physicians, which resulted in a partnership between the rep and the doctor. Regulations imposed on drug reps were limited in those days. It was understood that the ethical drug rep would be judicial in providing accurate information about his products, including indications, contra-indications, benefits, side-effects, and comparison with competitive products. The drug rep in those days was considered an important part of the healthcare team.

The requirements to become a drug representative were significantly more challenging than those for other sales endeavors. Lederle, the company I was employed by, required a degree in pharmacy or other heavily-science-oriented background, a demonstrated ability to communicate, as well as character traits of integrity and a desire to help others. After being evaluated by other pharmaceutical companies for a couple years, I was ultimately hired by Lederle (now Pfizer). Initial training was intense and, more importantly, continuous over a lifetime of employment. Lederle had the distinction of providing the most comprehensive training in the pharmaceutical industry. We had an in-depth knowledge of our drugs and how they reacted in the human body to cure disease. Physicians respected this and relied on us for advice in prescribing drugs.

My initial training consisted of extensive home study programs, two weeks of classroom training with my District Manager, field work with experienced representatives and District Manager, and finally, classroom training at our national training center in Pearl River, NY. With the extensive training that I received in the first two years of my employment, I felt very competent to call on doctors and provide them with the details of our drugs and how he/she could use them to treat their patients. Since most drug representatives provided the details of their drugs to doctors, the term "DETAIL MAN" became the trade name for us in the medical community. Again, I was very proud of the comprehensive training I had received that was the envy of the pharmaceutical industry. Little did I realize that in later years I would be involved in administering this training program to future reps on a national level.

My territory as a Lederle rep included parts of Norfolk, VA, most of eastern Virginia, and northeastern North Carolina. A typical day started around 7:00 a.m. by loading and organizing samples and literature from the garage to the trunk of my company-provided car. (Getting a new car every two years was one of the many benefits of the job.) I would have planned my day's itinerary the night before by organizing my doctor cards in the sequence that I planned to call on them. The doctor card contained essential information such as specialty, best time to see, receptionist's name, products used, results of the last call, etc. On a typical day, I would call on five to nine physicians, plus drug stores and hospitals in the area. Depending on how far my last call was from home, my day usually ended around 6-6:30 p.m. Some distant locations required overnight stays.

In the '60's and early '70's, many doctors, as well as drug reps, were smokers. The drug call provided a smoke break opportunity for the doctor, a time to catch up on local happenings, and also a time for the detail, i.e., sales call. On infrequent occasions, Joe Young, my District Manager, would ride with me to evaluate my performance and, if necessary, give me encouragement.

At least quarterly, the entire district of 12-14 reps would meet with Joe at a central location for our district meeting. I always looked forward to the meetings as a time to catch up with my fellow reps and to get new ideas on products and sales techniques. One of my fellow reps and good friends, Dave Bethune, competed constantly to lead the district in sales. We were both very good. Lederle ran a national sales contest each year called "Gold Cup," which rewarded top salespeople with a trip to a national resort, as well as the coveted "Gold Cup." While it was not easy to outsell my peers, I fell in love with the trips and recognition. At one time I held the Lederle record of four consecutive years of winning the "Gold Cup": quite a feat! "If you think you can, you can." During the year that I won the fourth consecutive Gold Cup, I also won the American Cyanamid Company's (Lederle parent company) top sales award, "The Golden Oval." This was a sales award for the top salesman in all divisions of American Cyanamid Co., which included pharmaceutical, agricultural, Shulton, Breck, Formica, and organic chemicals divisions. Beverly and I were treated royally at the Pierre Hotel overlooking Central Park in New York City. We dined at the best restaurants and attended several Broadway shows for several fun-filled days.

Dave Bethune and I remained friends throughout our careers, although the many positions we held did not always have us in close contact with each other. Dave became President of Lederle and later Executive Vice President of American Cyanamid. Now some 20+ years past our retirements, we remain friends and visit each other across the country. My years as a drug rep were some of the happiest years of my life; as I alluded to earlier in this story, regulations were very permissive in those days. I received a garage-full of drug samples every two months that I was able to dispense without accountability. Obviously, doctors were the intended recipients and that is where most of my samples were utilized. I did on occasion treat my family with antibiotics, steroids, or analgesics for minor respiratory illnesses, scrapes, cuts, itches, etc. My children used to say, "Daddy, how sick do we need to be to see a real doctor?" "Pretty sick," I would say. I was the first-line family doctor. The kids are all living today, with no known ill effects from my doctoring, so I guess I wasn't so bad after all.

After about five years as a sales rep, one day I got a call to be in Chicago the next day to meet with Jim Skinner, the Director of Sales. It turns out several other reps across the country were also called to Chicago. We all speculated about whether we were about to be fired or promoted and where we would be headed. As it turns out, I was being promoted to the position of Washington's District Manager. This would be my first of many relocations to the Washington, D.C. area. As Beverly often said, "We are being promoted into poverty!" The cost of living in the suburbs of Norfolk, VA, were considerably less than in the suburbs of Washington, D.C. We sold our three-bedroom brick rancher for $14,000 and had to pay $25,000 for a house in the D.C. area that was roughly comparable. The increase in my house payment just about took all my monthly increase in salary. Additionally, other living expenses in the area were higher. We rationalized that this was a sacrifice necessary to move up in the organization. "If you think you can, you can!" We all eventually learned to love living in Fairfax, VA, a suburb of D.C. Reid, Allison, and Stuart were all in top-notch schools, and we were living among the people that make our country tick - as one of our friends used to say, "People you just read about."

Life As a District Manager

The District Manager's job is probably the most critical and toughest job in the company, but also very rewarding. It is the first line of management between corporate headquarters and the field sales force. My district, the Washington District, included responsibility for fourteen sales representatives who covered all the metro area, a significant part of Maryland and West Virginia, as well as a slice of Virginia down to and including Richmond. In addition to managing these reps, I had personal responsibility for drug chain headquarters, like Peoples (now CVS), Drug Fair, and

Dart, who have all merged into what is now Rite Aid, Walgreens, and others.

The DM job in the early '70's was challenging to say the least. I did not have the benefit of cell phones, Internet, GPS, and many other technical advances we take for granted today. The job was, or seemed to be, 24/7. All communications with reps were in the evening since they were calling on doctors during the day. All communications with customers, the regional office, and headquarters personnel required the use of a pay phone when travelling, which was made more complicated by the fact that most days I was riding with one of my reps. My role as DM was to observe, train, counsel, encourage, and evaluate the reps' actions. Discretion was essential when calling on a doctor with a rep. It did not take many calls to determine if the rep had developed a favorable rapport with the doctor and office staff. Likewise, it was pretty easy to detect whether the rep was following his regular schedule or deliberately selecting specific doctors who were favorable towards him/her. A huge flag was raised with the consistent appearance of a rare or first-time call as displayed by the physician and staff. This was an indication that the rep had not been making regular calls on the physician. An ideal call frequency in those days was monthly. An exception was often determined by the physician who scheduled appointments with the drug rep. If the rep had established a good rapport with physicians during previous calls, this was a tremendous asset for him/her. The physician and staff were very cordial and accommodating to the rep as they were fully aware that the rep was being evaluated.

Evaluation/tutoring of the rep started prior to making the call. This included checking the company car for cleanliness, examination of the trunk and detail bag for organization and completeness of literature and samples, discussion of the call plan for the day, etc. My job was a combination of teaching, tutoring, counseling, critiquing, encouraging, and evaluating the rep's performance. Each physician call included a pre-call discussion and a post-call evaluation by the DM. If the rep was motivated, hard-working, and confident, he/she looked forward to a visit from the DM. The opposite was true for reps who were just going through the motions and doing the minimal amount of work to survive. In a nutshell, my job was to develop all reps to their fullest potential, identify top promotable reps, and provide opportunities for their growth. I also was responsible for identifying poor performers, as well as those that were not suitable for the job. In these cases, I worked with the regional director to plan their termination.

At least quarterly, I held a meeting for all representatives in the district to plan and prepare for the next three months' sales efforts. I would have previously attended, with the Regional Director and other DMs in the region, a meeting where the Regional Director would outline the company plan for the next three months. At the quarterly district meeting the reps would become familiar with the expected sales program, practice presentations (details), and hopefully leave the meeting well-prepared for the next three month's work. Most reps looked forward to this meeting. It was held at a central location in the district and offered time for the reps to socialize with each other on the night before the meeting. Reps were able to get ideas from their peers both informally during the socializing and formally during the meeting.

This meeting required a large amount of preparation time for me. It also provided me an opportunity to develop promising reps by assigning them specific sections of the meeting to conduct. The DM is always responsible for the outcome, so this meant coordinating with the selected rep to ensure that company plans and goals were implemented. The district meeting is the focal point of company meetings or 'where the rubber meets the road.' It is here that the ideas formulated at corporate headquarters are funneled down through national sales management, training and development, regional offices, and finally to the district level. This is the last level before the rep meets with the doctor, who is our customer.

In the event of new product launches, all representatives and managers may meet at a national location. This provides an opportunity for more excitement, fanfare, and for the reps to be exposed to regional and national management. One of the least desirable parts of the DM role is that darn biweekly report. This is a report of the past two weeks of activity directed to the VP of Sales with a copy to the Regional Director and other key national management. In addition to those copied, training and development personnel excerpted what they felt were key statements, ideas, and problems to forward to every level of corporate management. Realizing my thoughts and actions would be exposed to anyone who was anybody in the corporation, I spent laborious hours handwriting the document. Thankfully, Beverly laboriously typed it out on an old-fashioned 'hunt and peck' typewriter so that it would be readable. I considered it a plus if my idea or thought was excerpted for corporate management to review and follow-up on. It was noteworthy to be singled out among 60-70 DMs across the country. My comments were excerpted frequently for forwarding. ("If you think you can, you can.") DMs did not have secretaries; remember no cell phones, no email, no Internet. That meant that a lot of administrative work happened after standard work hours and on the weekends. I would have been up the creek if not for Beverly who acted as my secretary on a non-paid status. Taking telephone calls, orders, typing, etc., was a time-consuming experience. I was most thankful for her help.

Another responsibility I had was the recruiting, interviewing, hiring, and training of new reps. New representative training consisted of several days in a hotel room going over product information and procedures. This was initial training prior to formal training at company headquarters. Once I felt the rep was competent as measured by practiced sales presentations with me playing the doctor role, then came the real thing. We looked for older doctors with smaller practices for our trial runs. After several days of rep/DM calls, the rep was on their own in their territory. Constant follow-up in the first few weeks was imperative. It's a lonely feeling for a new rep to call on physicians and face the unexpected. They need much encouragement in the first few months of their new job. In fact, it's a 'make or break' time in their career. I served as a DM for five years, and while very challenging and time-consuming, I had just about decided I could do this for the rest of my career. It was not to be! Out of the blue one day, I got a call from Jim Skinner, Director of Sales. He said "Don, we need you in Pearl River, New York, to be Manager of our National Sales Training Department; don't ask any questions, just be in Pearl River next week." I, of course, had mixed emotions, as did Beverly. When we had moved from Norfolk, VA, to the Washington, D.C. area, her initial reaction had been "We are being promoted into poverty"; and now, "Looks like a similar situation moving from here to NY." In the early years of my career, her evaluation was not too far off base.

*Note: Many pharmaceutical reps elect to be career sales reps and forego promotion opportunities for good reason. If they are in a small town, particularly in the South, they are among the highest paid professionals in the area. They become pillars of the community and enjoy their status in their work. They are very happy with their current situation and see no reason to be promoted.

National Sales Training Manager

Lederle Laboratories was formed in 1909 in New York City by the former New York City Health Commissioner, Dr. Ernst Lederle. The laboratory was then a semi-rural farm in Pearl River, NY. Pearl River is in Rockland County across the Hudson River about 25 miles from New York City and about 30 miles south of the U.S. Military Academy at West Point. In the early days, Dr. Lederle bled farm horses to use their serum for making anti-toxins and vaccines. Throughout Lederle's history, the company remained a major supplier of vaccines in the U.S. as well as internationally. Most notable of these vaccines was oral polio vaccine, which eventually eradicated the dreaded disease of polio. Also in its early years, Lederle was a major supplier of penicillin for the WWII effort. What was then Lederle Laboratories is now Pfizer.

Once again, packed up with all we could cram into the car, Beverly, Reid, Allison, Stuart, and I left the busy, but comfortable life of the Washington Metro area for another unknown experience. We settled in River Vale, NJ, about five miles south of the Lederle campus in Pearl River, NY. The Lederle campus was an imposing complex with the main headquarters building being the focal point. The area was populated by numerous research, production, and manufacturing facilities. My office at the training center was in the main headquarters building. It was centrally located for the benefit of top management who wanted to observe and be with sales trainees as well as to observe and, if indicated, critique the trainers and training management. Welcome to the hot seat!! The closest comparison to this situation that I can think of is duty in the Pentagon. Here high-ranking colonels and one-star generals are constantly being observed and evaluated by two-, three-, and four-star generals along with the Secretary of Defense and other high-ranking civilians. My first reaction to this new job is "What have I gotten myself into? Can I handle this job?? Can I survive in this hot seat 24/7??" That old standby thought came back to me: "If you think you can, you can!"

My sales classes consisted of 30-40 new sales reps from across the country who had already received basic training from their District Managers. They had also gained about one year of experience working in the field.

By now they had been exposed to most situations that a drug rep would experience. The purpose of this advanced training was to learn more about the company and available resources, as well as to gain enhanced product knowledge from product managers and our medical staff. Also importantly, this provided an opportunity to tour our research and production facilities and to get to meet company management, who were in the process of identifying those reps with future management potential. My role as training manager was to organize and administer the program. This presented some challenges as my primary presenters/instructors were the department heads of major departments. I had to work around scheduling conflicts of the department heads as they were dealing with their primary responsibilities. I was the presenter for several sessions and often had to juggle my schedule to accommodate conflicts that arose with other presenters. The highlight of the training session was a final banquet at the local country club. In attendance at this event were the president, vice-president, and all major department heads. This gave the sales reps an opportunity to meet with upper management and an opportunity for management to mingle with the reps. The socializing after the banquet was conducted with an open bar. This often became one of the most challenging events to manage. On more than one occasion, I had to intervene when a young rep drank a little more than would be prudent in this environment.

The most challenging part of the event occurred when an occasional manager imbibed too much and created an embarrassing situation for himself as well as the company. To handle this individual, who was usually my senior, in a firm but diplomatic way presented situations which tested my competence as a manager. Some managers, if given the opportunity, would hang around all night to take advantage of free drinks while enjoying the social interaction with reps. Even though this event had been a company tradition for many years with the bar closing after the last manager left, I saw it as counter-productive to the company's best interest. After my recommendation to superiors, we agreed to close the bar at 10:00 p.m. Looking back, I viewed this action as one of my major contributions to the national training program. Needless to say, this also gave me a better opportunity to get a good night's sleep before going to work the next day.

In addition to sales rep classes, we held a training conference for new District Managers about once per year. The conference was held at an off-site resort area which offered luxurious accommodations as well as a quiet, private retreat for the participants. While I conducted many of the sessions, I also invited the company's top management along with other professionals who had expertise in management skills to present to the new DMs. The company considered the District Manager to be one of the most critical positions in the management structure; accordingly, they wanted new DMs to have the best possible training in the industry. In addition to administering training, I considered my two-year tour as national sales training manager to be superior training for me. During this period, I learned how the company operates from the corporate level. I also learned how to manage people who were my superiors. To the extent possible, I learned how to balance the egos of top managers while keeping the primary training role on track. The first tour of duty in the corporate headquarters, while demanding and stressful, proved to be one of the best growth periods of my career. It was also a life-expanding experience for Beverly and the kids. Being the southern genteel lady that she was, Beverly had to stretch to adapt to New Jersey ways. In time she soon fit right in with neighbors, friends, and other displaced Lederle wives. With their school, neighborhood, and church activities, Reid, Allison, and Stuart quickly became a part of the local scene.

Manager, Federal Government Affairs

It was the custom, Lederle's protocol, to give those managers who had been identified as potential higher level managers exposure to different aspects of the company. The time had arrived for me to move to a new endeavor. While serving as the Washington District Manager, I became acquainted with the Government Sales Manager, whose office was co-located with the regional office. I was intrigued that most of his effort dealt with U.S. military headquarters in the Washington, D.C., area and nationally. At the time, I was involved with the military as a Major in the U.S. Army Reserve. John Walker, the Government Sales Manager, continually complained that he was stretched too thin and needed an assistant. When the VP of Sales, Bob Sadah, asked me if I had any thoughts about a new assignment, I suggested Federal Government Sales Assistant as a viable option. Beverly, the kids, and I all liked living in the Washington, D.C., area, so that would be a good option professionally and personally. Needless to say, I was surprised as well as very pleased when I learned I would be going back to Washington as the Manager of Federal Government Affairs; yep, you heard it right!! – not as the assistant to the Government Sales Manager, but as his new boss!! This did not create a happy welcoming committee for me. Since John had been Lederle's exclusive authority on federal government for many years, this new arrangement was a major blow to his ego. It was the start of early retirement plans for him.

Because the scope of the operation was expanding, another position which would be reporting to me was announced simultaneously. It was to be filled by Fred Daussin. Fred was considered by Lederle to be one of the brightest employees in the company but somewhat deficient in people skills. Like John, he possessed an ego that drove his decisions and actions. I had worked for Fred in two previous roles when he was Director of Sales Education and Training and an assistant regional manager. Like most individuals who worked for Fred, my opinion of him was mixed – admiration for his skills and dislike for his methods. Welcome back to Washington!! An opportunity to exercise leadership skills while learning a new job or drown in the bruised egos of two demoted executives. I was determined to make the crippled system work. ("If you think you can, you can.")

My first challenge was to repair bruised egos and create the best possible working environment given the fact that John and Fred were two totally different personalities and not particularly friendly to each other. I started by letting each of them know that I personally admired their accomplishments in the company. I also tried to reassure them that their personal expertise was appreciated by the company; hence, their roles would not be diminished, but rather, an opportunity to focus their attention on specific areas which previously had been understaffed. John would keep his title, Government Sales Manager, and focus exclusively on the military and the veteran's administration. Fred would become Manager, National Accounts, and focus on U.S. Public Health Service, National Institutes of Health, CDC, U.S. State Department, and other agencies. I would be the Manager of Federal Government Affairs. In addition to establishing strategic goals and coordinating the total operation, my focus would be directed toward expanding Lederle government influence. This included new Lederle-sponsored programs, capitalizing on overseas military markets, and military commissary and exchange programs. While we each had areas of specialization, all of us were resources to corporate headquarters, regional offices, and the national sales force on federal sales issues. We each worked in the field with sales reps and managers, attended their meetings, and helped address problems/opportunities they were experiencing.

All was not 'peaches and cream' in the Federal Government Affairs office for some time. Although I gave it my best effort, bruised egos are hard to fix. We did, however, make significant progress due to our ability to pay closer attention to previously uncovered areas. Both John and Fred were considered among the industry's best by their customers. New innovations that I was able to implement impacted our federal sales in a very positive way. Prior to me being in charge of federal sales, John had established an award for the outstanding federal pharmacist of the year, called the Andrew Craigie Award. The award, which consisted of a sizeable honorarium and an engraved plaque, was presented each year at the annual meeting of the Association of Military Surgeons of the United States (AMSUS). (This is the national association of federal healthcare professionals). The awardee was selected by top federal pharmacy professionals. The award typically rotates between Army, Navy, Air Force, Veterans Administration, and U.S. Public Health Service. Being the sponsor of this award gave Lederle access to top decision-makers in federal pharmacy.

My goal was to hitch-hike on this successful idea, which I did over the next several years. In addition to the big annual meeting of AMSUS, the military services had a national meeting for physician specialties: OB/GYN, Urology, Family Practice, etc. My idea was to provide an award like the Andrew Craigie Award for the best paper presented at the annual specialty group meetings. The specialty group members would vote on the best paper presented at the meeting and notify me of the winner. After preparing the plaque, I would arrange to present the plaque and an honorarium at the winner's local hospital. Accompanying me for the presentation would be the local Lederle rep who called on the hospital. This was a win/win/win for Lederle, the specialty group, and the hospital. Often the hospital commander would arrange for hospital staff to participate with photo ops, speeches, etc. Most importantly, the local Lederle rep was recognized, and his/her access to the hospital and staff was significantly enhanced. I established this Lederle-sponsored award program, which was endorsed and appreciated by the military services and the specialty groups alike. Included were the key specialties which were candidates for the use of Lederle products:

OB/Gyn, Family Practice, Urology, and Dermatology. This gave me the opportunity to attend their meetings, mingle with the physicians, and most importantly, enhance accessibility for the local Lederle rep. In addition to attending their meetings, I was able to display and discuss our products with them.

Another innovation that I implemented was opening the market to Lederle with military exchanges and commissaries. During these years, Lederle was becoming a significant player in the over-the-counter market with Stress Tabs and Centrum vitamins. At the time, Lederle sold only to pharmacies - no grocery or other outlets. I felt the military resale market offered a great new potential for Lederle. I approached my boss, Bob Sadah, VP of Sales, about the idea. He turned it down flatly, saying we would upset our pharmacy customers if we sold to other trade classes. Not willing to forego the opportunity, after several more discussions with Bob, I finally convinced him that military commissaries and exchanges were not in conflict with pharmacies. Moreover, military personnel and dependents did not get vitamins from military pharmacies, but from exchanges and commissaries. Eventually, he reluctantly gave me the ok to proceed. Wow - did I have a lot to learn! First, I learned that military resale business is done through brokers, not direct. I researched and employed the largest military broker in the business, VH Monet Co. in Smithfield, VA.

This proved to be a mistake!! Despite their stellar reputation, in the big picture, our line was so small that their representatives did not give it appropriate attention. Back to the drawing-board; after more research and trying to marry our line with a more specialized company, I selected the George E. Abbott Co. of Chester, CT. We enjoyed a long-time, successful business relationship with them for many years. Progress was slow at first. I remember we only sold $50,000 worth the first year. Over the years, the business became substantial.

I previously mentioned my activity with AMSUS. One of my honors was being elected to serve as Chairman, Sustaining Members AMSUS. The Sustaining Members were the approximately 200 companies that did business with federal medical facilities. As Chairman, I was the industry representative, which gave me membership on the Executive Committee of AMSUS. The Executive Committee consisted of the Surgeon General of the US Public Health Service, as well as the Surgeon Generals of the U.S. Army, U.S. Navy, and U.S. Air Force. Additionally, the Secretary of the Veterans Administration was a member of the Executive Committee. This position gave me the opportunity to voice the industry position on federal healthcare issues. I was pleased that I got to know the leadership of federal healthcare personally. These contacts helped me professionally on several occasions.

Another highlight of my federal medical involvement was establishing Lederle's product promotion at overseas military bases. During the Cold War, Germany alone had 250,000 U.S. military personnel in the country. With dependents, this brought the U.S. population in Germany to about 750,000 that were treated in seven U.S. military hospitals and numerous medical clinics. England and Italy, with significantly smaller numbers, were nevertheless still important.

Due to limited resources, my primary focus was Germany. I set up a system for direct communication between military hospitals in Germany and my office, which facilitated rapid processing of emergency orders. We also made an annual trip to Germany to call on physicians in military hospitals to promote our products. While we tested calls in England and Italy, we quickly discovered our best return, given limited time and resources, would be in Germany. The entire country of Germany is about the size of the state of Georgia. Since the hospitals and military bases were relatively concentrated, our travel time was limited, providing more time to be with the customer. I made several trips personally. My government accounts manager or I made at least one annual trip. To say the least, the logistics of these trips was challenging. This was before the era of cell phones, Internet, GPS, etc., and language barriers provided additional complications. Since U.S. military bases were relatively close to each other, we could find them rather easily. At that time, all U.S. vehicles had green USA license tags. The rule was: if you get lost, follow the green. Once on base with friendly English-speaking people, we could get clear directions to the next location. The relationships we established not only helped Lederle product usage in Germany, but also continued when the physicians returned to the U.S.

Looking back, I marvel at the challenges and accomplishments the overseas military experiences afforded me. Quite an unlikely experience for a boy growing up on an isolated small farm in southwest Virginia. "If you think you can, you can." After returning from an overseas trip and headed to the grocery store with Beverly, she would advise me, "Slow down, turn left here, there's a stop sign." My response, "Beverly, I have just driven all over Germany, where I couldn't read the signs, didn't speak the language, had no advice, and yet I found my way. I think I can find my way to the neighborhood grocery store."

During the early years of the federal government affairs office operation, we made a significant impact relative to our pharmaceutical competitors. The federal government published annual sales by supplier as measured by the federal supply schedules. Lederle was always in the top three or four companies, and one year we were #1. To put that into perspective, Lederle was never that near the top in the civilian sector. Of course, I was proud. "If you think you can, you can."

Don as a very young and happy boy

Early picture of Don and his sister, Joyce Ann, with their parents

Don as a young man

Don in front of his grandfather's home where he spent much of his youth

**Don and Beverly
in early marriage years**

**Don, Beverly, and Reid when Don was a senior
in the VA Tech Corps of Cadets**

**1st Lt Don Sowder, Aide de Camp for General
William Purnell, Commander, 29th Infantry Division**

**Captain Don Sowder (2nd from left) supervising one of
his 105mm Howitzer gun crews, 111th Field Artillery**

Don and Beverly - proud grandparents of West Point graduate, John Sowder

Don with a wagonload of grandkids

Don and Beverly with two of their VA Tech Corps of Cadets scholarship recipients

Don's induction into Ut Prosim Society by President of VA Tech and Chairman of the Board of Regents

Don and family members in front of his North Carolina beach house

Don enjoying fishing at his Corolla, NC, home

Don's initial stages of gazebo construction

Don's completed gazebo

The Lederle Gold Cup Club

Membership in the Lederle Gold Cup Club is a distinction earned by those men whose sales achievement puts them in the top five percent of their respective Regions. Lederle salesmen who win this most sought after award place themselves in an outstanding group of men.

The 23-year history of Gold Cup, which started in 1947, has seen much hard work, planning and superior individual effort. The driving urge to win, to achieve far beyond what was expected or required, has been the common ingredient of all Gold Cuppers.

The Gold Cup winner, standing in the spotlight on award night, may only partially hear the applause and recital of his past year's achievements. The oration, warm handshake and cup confirm the recognition of his achievement. The participant will never forget the thrill of winning and will gauge his future efforts by a higher standard – that of a Gold Cup Winner.

DON SOWDER — RICHMOND DISTRICT — SOUTHEAST REGION

Four consecutive Gold Cups - a tremendous feat! Don also "rang the bell" by being chosen a Golden Oval winner in 1969. His excellent customer rapport has resulted in continued sales of Achromycin products to his hospitals in the face of generic competition. He also proved to be an "iron man" by selling over $9,000 of Ferro Sequels.

DON SOWDER accepts his fourth Gold Cup from Lederle General Manager, BORDEN PUTNAM. Sharing this honor with DON are CLIFF SIVERD, VERN REGER and DR. J. R. BOURLAND.

8

Don receiving the coveted Lederle Gold Cup Award for national sales achievement

Don (center) with his Lederle national hospital sales force

Colonel Sowder as Inspector General IMA U.S. Military Academy West Point

Don presenting Andrew Craigie Award to Rear Admiral Church for Outstanding Federal Pharmacy Programs

Family picture - Don's children and grandchildren 2006

Don with former VA Governor and US Senator, George Allen

Don's campaign booth

**Campaign literature for re-election Chesterfield
County Board of Supervisors (2007)**

Don and current wife, Mary

Don and Mary with her two daughters, their husbands, and the grandchildren in Texas (2022)

National Hospital and Government Sales Manager

After having served as Manager of the federal government sales efforts for five years, I was very confident in my success, very comfortable in the job, and loving my work. With this as a background, my phone rang one morning; it was Larry Tilton, Director of Sales. "Hello, Don; we need you in Wayne, NJ, to be the National Hospital Sales Manager." My response, "Larry, I am very happy here and making good progress, but I still have ideas for future projects in the government." "That's well and good," countered Larry, "but we want you in Wayne." Realizing the inevitable, I said, "Ok, Larry, but I would still like to have the government sales operation report to me." That turned out to be an easy sell. Larry said, "Ok", and once again we were off to Yankee land. My new title became National Manager, Hospital and Government Sales. On my previous northern assignment, I worked at the Lederle facility in Pearl River, NY. This new assignment was located at the American Cyanamid corporate headquarters in Wayne, NJ. All Lederle top management was now co-located with other divisions of Cyanamid. My office was in a beautiful, circular building that overlooked a large lake. The park-like setting for the complex was very pastoral and inviting – not at all like the typical concept of the NJ scene. My office was between Larry Tilton, Director of Sales, and George White, Asst. Director of Sales. The space we occupied was very busy as the focal point of

Lederle's national sales operation. After getting the family settled into a nice community in Wycoff, NJ, I was in for a totally new experience. Except for the government sales office, which reported directly to me, the major portion of my job was as a staff member, rather than direct management. Across the country we had ten hospital District Managers and approximately 140 hospital specialty representatives. The hospital District Managers reported to Regional Directors with a dotted line (staff) relationship to me. Stated more succinctly, I was their contact point in the corporate office.

My first action was to find a person to replace me in the Washington government sales office. Marty Cuddyre had been a successful sales rep with a large contingent of government customers. He was also a very successful District Manager and Regional Director, who was ready for a new challenge. He fit the bill and proved over time to be a good selection for the job. After a few weeks of getting his feet wet in this new environment, Marty required limited supervision. The bulk of my time, therefore, was devoted to the hospital sales force. The primary challenge for me was learning to motivate, encourage, advise, and critique the hospital District Managers in a staff reporting relationship rather than a direct reporting relationship. Since the Regional Directors had five combination districts, which represented the bulk of their region, and only one hospital district, the hospital District Managers tended to look to me for direction and support. That made the staff relationship a bit more tolerable. As a part of my duties, I worked with hospital representatives across the country. This kept me tuned in to what was happening in the field. All District Managers, including hospital District Managers, had quarterly meetings with their reps. I attended one of these meetings across the country each quarter. This gave me the opportunity to get to know the manager better and to meet the reps. It also gave me the opportunity to deliver the headquarters perspective directly.

On an annual basis, the Director of Sales and Asst. Director of Sales traveled to the regional offices with the specific purpose of evaluating the Regional Director and District Managers in a formal performance evaluation. Larry Tilton, my boss, Director of Sales, asked me to join them on this visit for my evaluation of hospital District Managers. This was a learning experience for me, as well as a confirmation of the challenges presented by direct report versus dotted line report style management. In most cases, the Regional Director's and my evaluation of the hospital District Manager coincided – but not always. In these times, I felt like the boxer with one hand tied behind his back. I did learn a lot about leadership and management by observing my superiors, as well as some of the most experienced and professional Regional Directors in the pharmaceutical industry. During the time I served as National Hospital and Government Sales Manager, I visited most parts of this country numerous times and was fortunate to be a part of a great corporate sales and marketing management team.

One of the highlights of my experience in this job was the introduction of a new hospital antibiotic, Pipracil. This included a national launch meeting and all the background corporate planning to make the launch meeting a success. Of course, the critical part of the success was all the scientists, researchers, physicians, and others that developed and tested the antibiotic. The meeting planning was the responsibility of the marketing department, but as the Hospital Sales Manager, I would be the host of the meeting. We invited key corporate executives, as well as key infectious disease experts in the U.S., marketing executives, and others to be speakers at the launch meeting, which was to be held in Dallas, TX. We established numerous teaching sessions manned by experts, which all the reps visited to increase their knowledge in dealing with surgeons. In order to assist the reps in identifying with the role of a surgeon, we decided to order surgical scrubs for all our hospital reps to wear throughout all the launch meeting activities. It was my job to open the meeting with a motivational message, introduce speakers, and facilitate activities. The meeting was a success from the standpoint of our national hospital sales force getting together and leaving the meeting with the knowledge and resources to make Pipracil a major new antibiotic for surgical prophylaxis and in the treatment of hospital-acquired infections. In time, it became an antibiotic of choice for many infections by many physicians.

During the time I served as manager of hospital sales, we were starting to increase our line of oncology products. It was also a time when drug reps were becoming more specialized due to the highly technical nature of products and their usage. It was in this environment that top Lederle management decided that growth in the oncology market would be dependent upon having a highly specialized sales force. Up to this point in time, we had a few hospital reps that were focusing on oncology. The future of Lederle's oncology sales was destined for a dramatic change. Management made the decision that I would be the guy to make it happen. With all its challenges, the good news was that this job did not require a family change of location.

National Oncology Manager

I was finally settled in with hospital sales doing well and government sales exceeding expectations. Since oncology was an entirely new venture and no one in the company had experience in this area, my guidance and marching orders for this new venture were very sparse. As I recall, the absolutes I received as guidance were as follows: 1) every sales representative must be a trained oncology pharmacist or a PharmD (Doctor of Pharmacy),

2) every rep will be equipped with a laptop computer and trained with its use, 3) I must initially hire enough reps to cover the entire country with three districts (approximately 36 reps) and three District Managers. This was the first time I had had the challenge of starting a new operation from scratch. It would not be the last. The primary challenge for me was that I knew virtually nothing about oncology and oncology treatment protocols. In terms of my knowledge of computers, it was nil. After all, this was occurring in the late '80's and early '90's when laptop computers were still in their infancy. In fact, very few practicing oncologists had access to laptop computers, particularly in semi-rural areas. While I was a skeptic on the idea of equipping the oncology sales force with laptop computers, it turned out to be an innovative idea.

The treatment of cancer, for the most part, is not with a single drug; rather, several drugs used in combination. In the best-case scenario, the treatment for the most part is experimental. Oncologists, unlike other physician specialties, confer with their peers on most every patient. They rely primarily on established protocol treatment options. These protocols are constantly changing, which requires a high level of communication within the oncology community. The idea of equipping the oncology sales rep with a computer was innovative at the time. It gave the rep increased access to the oncologist inner circle. The idea was that the rep could go into the oncologist's office and connect him by the computer to the National Cancer Institute or other information sources. This was a much more efficient method of analyzing treatment protocols than the telephone or journal articles. The idea was great!! The implementation was much more challenging; more on that later.

The oncology sales operation was to be offsite - not in the corporate headquarters. Among my first actions was to set up an oncology headquarters office with staff. The model for this setup was our current regional office setup. I ultimately established an office in the next town over from the corporate headquarters and hired Marie Lehive as Secretary, Kathy Hurtado, an oncology pharmacist, as Trainer, and Herb Jacobs as Administrative Assistant. We started with a phone, a table, and folding chairs. Eventually, we ended up with all the furniture, communication equipment, and technology to support a nationwide operation. Simultaneously, I started the significant task of hiring the sales force. First, of course, was hiring three District Managers who would assist in hiring the reps. The Eastern District Manager would be Joanne Naso, the Central District Manager would be Keith Gates, and the Western District Manager would be Randy Lewis. The District Managers and I scoured the country looking for the very best applicants we could find. The ones ultimately hired came from academic settings, competitive oncology sales forces, and a few from our own hospital sales force. The selection was a delicate balance! It is very difficult to identify individuals who are highly skilled academically and who also have the necessary personality traits and sales skills to be successful. Further complicating the challenge is the information that can be exchanged between the rep and the physician. General drug reps and hospital reps are only allowed to promote drugs for indications which have been studied and approved by the FDA. These indications and contraindications are spelled out specifically in the package circular that accompanies the drug. On the other hand, most drugs used for cancer treatment have vague indications not approved by the FDA and many are used experimentally in combination with other drugs. The very nature of cancer, which is frequently terminal, puts the oncologist in a difficult position when determining the therapy that will be used. Hence, collaboration with his/her peers and utilization of drug protocols that offer the best chance of success become the standard. The bottom line is that, often, drugs used by oncologists to treat cancers have neither formal indications nor approval by the FDA. One can readily see that the role the oncology rep plays is at a much different level than that of the general drug sales representative; so much for the challenge of identifying those individuals that have the unique academic credentials and personalities to be successful oncology sales representatives.

Now, back to the laptop computers; my gut feeling about them was that reps would be consumed with trying to figure out how to use them. After all, the technology was relatively new, and the capability of the laptop was very limited in comparison to today's laptops. Even a simple task like sending an email was complicated for new users. I was right – despite our rudimentary training by the one or two computer geeks in our organization, reps were spending valuable time trying to figure out the computer rather than spending time with the customer. It took a few weeks for some reps to be able to communicate with our office via computer. As the technology improved, as well as the skill of the user, the use of laptops was one of the major innovations for the oncology sales force. The Lederle oncology sales force was a pioneer in the pharmaceutical industry in using laptops. The Lederle oncology sales rep was welcomed in many oncologists' offices based on the service they could provide. A typical sales call might be a computer session shared between the oncology rep, the oncologist, and the National Institutes of Health detailing a new treatment protocol for a specific type of cancer. Of course, the rep tried to focus these sessions to protocols that used our products. The primary products we were promoting included Methotrexate, Calcium Leucovorin, Novantrone, and Thio Tepa. Our rep, in general, was a facilitator. He/she connected the oncologist customer with the researchers who had established effective treatment protocols using our products.

At the hospital level, all oncologists on staff had frequent meetings called "tumor boards". Attendance at "tumor boards" often included other physician specialties or specialized medical personnel. The purpose of the "tumor board" was to review a specific patient's cancer type and develop a consensus for the best treatment for this patient. Often, oncology reps were permitted to attend these meetings due to the expertise or the resources that the rep could provide. A general drug rep would not be permitted to attend these types of medical meetings in a hospital setting. The fact that the oncology rep was a trained oncology pharmacist, or a Doctor of Pharmacy, moved them to a higher level of acceptance by the medical community. While cancer patients are treated in all types of settings, including community and general hospitals, a few major facilities across the country develop the protocols for treatment of most cancers. Some of the most notable facilities include MD Anderson Cancer Center in Houston, TX, Memorial Sloan Kettering Hospital in NYC, Dana Farber Cancer Institute in Boston, and the Mayo Clinic in various locations, as well as other cancer centers. All oncologists and our oncology reps stayed tuned in to new information and protocols from these prestigious institutions. In addition to our oncology products, our reps promoted our powerful IV antibiotics, Pipracil and Zosan. Cancer patients are immuno-compromised and subject to bacterial infection. Antibiotics are used both prophylactically and for treatment of cancer patients.

I eventually expanded the oncology sales force to five districts of approximately 75 reps total. As oncology is not a heavily populated specialty, even with our expanded force most reps were covering at least one state, and some were covering two or more states. This meant extensive travel and time away from family for the reps and even more so for District Managers.

While overall I enjoyed the challenge of setting up a new operation, this was my least favorite job during my 30+ years with Lederle. The nature of the job, i.e., product knowledge and selling techniques, was very different. In all my previous jobs I considered myself to be as technically knowledgeable, if not more so, than my subordinates; also in previous jobs, I knew the customer types, and I had the skills required to influence their favorable action for our products. In the current scenario, I never felt confident in evaluating my subordinates or providing advice. In fact, rather than being the expert, my subordinates were the experts. During this time, I gained a great appreciation for the fact that it is very difficult to find individuals who excel in technical abilities and who also possess the personality traits to be a good salesperson. It was also during this time that my upper management was in a state of upheaval with executives brought in from outside the company becoming more prominent. The company was also in a pre-takeover mode by the American Home Products Corporation. All of this added to a sense of frustration and a somewhat stressful experience.

As I was nearing a potential retirement age, I had no interest in working for our eventual new parent company, Wyeth Laboratories. Events evolved with some "political moves" by me that made it possible to return to northern Virginia, a suburb of Washington, D.C., and my first love – government sales. This I did!!! "If you think you can, you can."

Lederle – The End

With the American Home Products takeover moving at a fast pace, I was very happy to be back in Washington. I was offered a buyout of my remaining tenure by my superior, VP of Sales. However, my old friend, Dave Bethune, now President of Lederle, called and encouraged me to stick around for a while. He said, "Wyeth may need you to assist in the merger of the two government sales operations." I agreed when he said, "I can increase your base pay which will then help in calculating your retirement annuity."

I settled in to running the government business which I had developed years earlier. The business had grown significantly, and I now had six managers reporting to me. It had been a long-time policy of Lederle to send

Lederle managers to me who had been a big asset to the company but now had no positions and were nearing retirement. With the takeover by Wyeth in the works, this policy was in full play. In addition to my secretary, Pat Robinson, whom I had hired many years earlier, and my administrative assistant, Jerry Penn, a retired Navy Lt. Commander, I had six managers on my staff: Dave Brandstetter, Southeast Government Manager, a retired South-Atlantic Regional Director; Don Caldwell, Southwest Government Manager, a retired Central Regional Director; Marty Cuddyre, Gulf Coast Government Manager, a retired West Coast Regional Director; Ron Schoch, Central Government Manager, a retired Detroit District Manager; Pete Johnson, West Coast Government Manager, retired West Coast Hospital District Manager; Dan Brupbacher, South Central Government Manager.

Managing this group and maintaining their enthusiasm and productivity in this environment was challenging to say the least. As the takeover started ramping up, I was given directions to terminate, retire or help transfer all members of the staff. Ultimately, Don Caldwell, Marty Cuddyre, Ron Schoch, Pete Johnson, and Dan Brupbacher accepted jobs with Wyeth Pharmaceuticals. Pat Robinson, Jerry Penn, and Dave Brandstetter were retired from Lederle Laboratories. I was the lone person left in the government sales office. I was awaiting a call from Wyeth for me to help with the transition. That call never came. I was the consummate executive with no mission other than to disperse office furniture and close the operation. To say things were quiet and boring is an understatement. In an attempt to stay in the loop and keep up with what was happening at headquarters, I called in frequently. One by one, I was told, Mr. Goodwin is no longer here, Mr. White is no longer here, Mr. Tilton is no longer here, etc., etc. The final straw came when I called my friend, Dave Bethune, and I was told Mr. Bethune is no longer here. I had previously received directions to get rid of all office furniture; I was given no directions on where to ship, no accountability, just told to get rid of it. I gave most of it away to friends and former employees for just picking it up. I still have my office desk in my home. Finally, all my calls were going unanswered. I called the personnel department, and a secretary answered. I said, "Hello, my name is Don Sowder." In a confused voice she said, "This place is closed down, I'm the only one here, but how can I help you?" I said, "I was just calling in to check on my raise." After a few moments of silence, she said, "Mr. Sowder, our records show you as retired!" I said, "I know that, but I'm just checking on my raise that Mr. Bethune promised me." She said, "I am confused, but I will forward this information to my Wyeth counterpart." I could just visualize how she responded to her husband that evening when he asked, "How was your day?" Needless to say, I was surprised, but happy, when my final check included a raise. Yes, it did help in calculating my retirement pay. No doubt, in the confusion of the merger, the normal procedure of signoff by several top managers for raises at my pay level was bypassed. No people, no furniture, phone line dead, I took down the Lederle sign, closed the door, and thought, "What a wonderful ride for the last thirty years! If you think you can, you can!"

Interesting, Unlikely Happenings Along the Way

In my official capacity with Lederle Laboratories I was involved in numerous meetings throughout the U.S. One of these meetings with other Lederle managers occurred in Lake Tahoe, Nevada. While I do not recall the nature of this meeting, the evening dinner event turned out to be outside the ordinary for me. My fellow managers had made a reservation at a dinner theatre where the famous American sweetheart singer-actress, Debbie Reynolds, was to be the headliner. It occurred to me that Debbie had lived for a short period of time in Roanoke, VA, near where I was raised. After she had been married to another famous singer and actor, Eddie Fisher, Debbie married a Roanoke native she had met in Las Vegas, Richard Hamlett. She lived with him high on a mountain in a mansion in Roanoke.

While not tipping off my peers, I came up with the thought that it would be really special if Debbie would recognize our group during the evening. I felt the chance of this to be next to none, yet I quickly developed a plan.

("If you think you can, you can!") Having been raised in the Roanoke area, I knew that the small city of Roanoke, VA, was not widely known, so I wrote a note on a piece of scratch paper which essentially said the following: "Debbie, my name is Don Sowder. I am here in the audience with a group of Lederle managers. Probably you and I are the only people here that ever heard of Roanoke, VA. If it is appropriate, I would be most appreciative if you could recognize our group." Upon entering the dinner theatre, I asked the Maitre D' if he could get my note to Debbie. He was not very encouraging but assured me he would try.

Even though the dinner theatre was relatively small with an attendance of 100 to 150, I had minimal hope that Debbie would get the note and even less hope that she would honor the request. Our dinner table was just at the edge of the stage. I had not alerted my fellow managers to the note I had written. We enjoyed our dinner very much and were eagerly looking forward to the show.

After a warm-up group of entertainers performed, the great Debbie Reynolds, dressed to the nines and with her charming persona, finally appeared on stage. After she sang two or three numbers and captivated the audience as only Debbie could do, one of my life's most interesting experiences occurred. Debbie, shading her eyes from the bright lights, looked out into the audience saying "Is Don here? Is my friend Don Sowder out there?" I am unable to describe the looks of amazement and disbelief on the faces of my friends. Being close to the stage, we easily got her attention, and she kindly and graciously acknowledged our group. They, of course, were eager to find out about my connection with Debbie. I jokingly and unconvincingly explained that we were long-lost friends. In reality, our only connection was that she and I were probably the only ones in the house who had ever heard of Roanoke, VA. So much for my connection with the famous Debbie Reynolds!!

Following is another example of an unexpected, interesting happening along the way. The Department of Veterans Affairs, located at Vermont Avenue near The White House in Washington, D.C., was one of my largest customers. I called on the headquarters routinely, at least once a month. Among the key people I called on was Albert Bryant, the Chief of Pharmacy Service for V.A. pharmacies nationwide. Al was also a general in the U.S. Army Reserve. In addition to our professional relationship, we became good friends. The V.A. system, then as well as now, relied on Congressional allocations to fund the system. The Chairman of the Senate Veterans Affairs Committee at that time was Senator Sonny Montgomery from Mississippi. He played a key role in determination of funding for The Veterans Administration.

My friend, Al, informed me that Senator Montgomery was having a birthday, and that The Department of

Veterans Affairs would like to assist in arranging a small birthday party for him. The Department, of course, had no money available and wondered if I could help out financially. As the V.A. was a key customer, I agreed to provide some support from my Lederle promotional fund. The party was to be held in one of the Senate office buildings, and I was invited. At first I had not planned to attend, but since I was working late in D.C. on the night of the party, I decided to go. After working my way through several levels of security, I began to realize that this was a very special event. When I finally arrived at the room where the party was being held, I discovered it was a very small room - intended to host an intimate gathering. Attendees included the "Who's Who" of the Washington elite at the time. My first reaction was thinking, "Wow! I am a bit low in the hierarchy of this guest list, but I am going to mingle, given the small number of attendees." Among the notables present in addition to Senator Montgomery was then Secretary of the V.A., Anthony Principi; then Speaker of the House, Tip O'Neal; then Attorney General of the U.S., Edwin Mease; and topping the list was then Vice-President, George Bush, Sr.

I can envision even now the informality and the genuine friendliness of the gathering; I met and exchanged greetings with all the distinguished guests. Could I ever forget when Vice-President Bush came up to me and said, "Hi, I am George Bush," and I replied, "Nice to meet you, sir; I am Don Sowder."? All of the guests continued to enjoy exchanging small talk, and Senator Montgomery enjoyed the attention given to him by all as the birthday guest of honor. I never learned whether this event influenced his positive impact on funding for The Veterans Administration. Whether it did or not, this small gathering represented the way Washington, D.C., works. You can imagine how surprised my wife, Beverly, was when I called to tell her about my extraordinary evening!!

Fired and Sued in My First Post-Lederle Job

In those days, a popular method of promoting pharmaceutical products was called peer influence meetings. In this scenario, pharmaceutical companies invited physicians to attend small group dinner meetings to discuss specific diseases and options for treatment.

One of the lead companies which conducted this type of event was Boron-Lepore. Lederle had been one of their primary clients. With the merger of Lederle into Wyeth Laboratories, many former Lederle executives, including me, were looking for ways to continue using their pharmaceutical industry skills. Many of these former Lederle executives had already been employed by Boron-Lepore and were leading discussions at the physician dinner meetings around the country. Included in former Lederle employees were John Goodwin, former VP of Sales; Jim Bacon, former Regional Director,

Rocky Mountain Region; Dwight McCoy, former Director, Education Services and Training; in addition to others.

Now that I no longer had Lederle responsibilities, I was looking for opportunities to continue employment in the pharmaceutical industry. I ultimately joined the Boron-Lepore team and found it to be a unique, challenging, and enjoyable way to continue my pharmaceutical service. In this role, the Boron-Lepore employee was the moderator of the physician dinner meeting discussions. Several weeks before I would be assigned as moderator of a program, I would have received study materials from the pharmaceutical company I would be representing. I was expected to become an expert on the disease entity/product that I would be promoting.

On a typical week, I received an itinerary which included the company/product that I would be promoting in addition to the cities for the events and hotel reservations where I would be staying. Also included were airline tickets and rental car reservations, the anticipated attendees, as well as other logistical data. The dinner meetings were held at a hotel or restaurant, and the preference was to host small groups of 12-15 physicians in order to facilitate discussions. The meetings were in a different city every day. A typical weekly itinerary might be to fly to NYC on Monday to conduct a meeting that night; on Tuesday, fly to Boston and conduct another evening meeting; on Wednesday, fly to Philadelphia for another one; on Thursday, fly to Cleveland, conducting the final meeting of the week. On Friday, I would fly home (no meetings were scheduled on Fridays). The meetings were all dinner meetings. We conducted/moderated the programs while the physicians ate. We learned this to be the best method for maximum attention of the physicians. If we held a meeting prior to dinner, physicians became impatient awaiting the food; if we held the meeting after the dinner, the physicians mysteriously had emergency calls, prior appointments, etc. We were able to keep their attention while they were eating. Typically, in the hotel conference room setting, the food would be in the back of the room for the physicians to serve themselves buffet style. In restaurant settings, they ordered from a preset menu.

My role as moderator was to arrive at the meeting site in ample time to ensure the meeting room was set up correctly and to coordinate with the hotel to ensure an adequate amount of food would be available to accommodate the expected number of attendees. Of course, the most important function was to conduct the meeting. This included providing an overview of the topic to be discussed and leading the discussion to keep the primary focus on track. The idea was to identify physicians who were knowledgeable and had had favorable experiences with the product being discussed in the treatment of the disease entity. As moderator, I had to be an expert on the product and able to answer questions. The most successful meetings, however, were those where one or more physician advocates helped sell the product by discussing their successful clinical experience with other attending physicians. If no attendees had experience with the product, the moderator's role became much more critical and challenging. Predicting an accurate number of attendees was always a challenge. Some physicians who had committed to attend did not show up, and others who had not been invited by the company did show up. This was most notable when an invited staff physician chose to invite his residents without notifying the company. My role as moderator was to welcome all physicians and to facilitate space and food requirements as necessary. In my approximately two years in this role, I experienced meetings where no physicians showed up and others where thirty more than anticipated showed up. In either case, I made adjustments as needed. ("If you think you can, you can").

During my time with Boron-Lepore, I conducted programs all over the country from the Mid-Atlantic to the Northwest, and in addition, from the Northeast to the deep South and throughout the Central U.S. Meetings were conducted in large cities and mid-size towns, including major metro areas as well as more semi-rural settings. To say the least, I saw a good part of the U.S. and visited most major cities, often several times. The physician specialists that I worked with most frequently were family practitioners, OB-GYNs, surgeons, dermatologists, and anesthesiologists. I enjoyed the challenge of learning about new products and becoming comfortable with helping physicians learn more about them. I particularly appreciated the opportunity to visit virtually every part of this country. In the process, I met some very fine and appreciative physicians, as well as some who just showed up for the food. Imagine that!! On one occasion, I was in the process of closing down and packing up my materials when a lone pediatrician showed up. She said, "I was not able to attend your lecture, but thought you would have food left over for me to take home to my family." I don't think she was living in poverty, but she surely acted like it.

One day out of the blue, I got a call from Sander Flaum, CEO of Robert A. Becker, a medical advertising agency in NYC. Sander was a former Lederle colleague. He said, "I want to set up a separate division in my company to run peer influence meetings. Would you do that for me?" I promised to get back to him. I always like new challenges, and, in this case, it was substantially more rewarding financially. Based on commitment from Sander for total autonomy and whatever resources I needed, I accepted the assignment. Here I am for the second time starting an organization from scratch with no guidance except promises of whatever support I needed.

My employment arrangement with Boron-Lepore was as an independent contractor. I had neither an employment nor non-compete agreement with them. I prepared a letter of resignation for Boron-Lepore. In the meantime, I received notification from Boron-Lepore that I was fired immediately. I was also notified that they would see me in court. Apparently, the word of my intentions was leaked, and this represented a potential threat to their business. Within a few weeks after some conversation, the whole issue disappeared.

While I continued to maintain my personal residence in the Washington, D.C., area, my primary work location was now in Manhattan. This required commuting from the D.C. area to Manhattan and hotel nights in the Big Apple. An airline offering hourly flights in both directions between NYC and D.C. came in quite handy.

Vice-President/Managing Director, Peer Perspectives

Working in NYC was an interesting and exciting time at this stage of my life. While I had spent several years just across the Hudson River from NYC with Lederle Laboratories, Manhattan was a world away from the quiet New Jersey towns that I had lived and worked in. My New York work location was at 50th and Broadway – right in the middle of the action of mid-town Manhattan.

I learned much about the hectic pace of Manhattan during the two years that I was headquartered there. After initially being somewhat timid in trying to cope, I actually learned to like the environment. I learned that Manhattan people are normal people just like everybody else regardless of where they lived and worked. One significant difference was the normal workday, which started at 9:00 a.m. and often ended at 9:00 p.m.

Robert A. Becker Co. was one of the largest medical advertising agencies in NYC and was located on the 24th floor of the Paramount building. Becker had approximately 200 employees with most employees assigned to an account team that developed advertising campaigns for their pharmaceutical company clients. Sander Flaum, the CEO, had a goal of expanding services offered by the firm. This resulted in his asking me to join the firm with the idea of setting up a peer influence group as a part of the Robert A. Becker enterprise. As previously pointed out, I had worked with Sander at Lederle Laboratories, so he knew my capabilities and felt comfortable in giving me total autonomy in designing and setting up this new venture. Sander's remarks to me at the outset were "You do what you need to do to make this a successful venture, and I will provide you the resources you need." This was the birth of what became Peer Perspectives, the peer influence group that I developed and initially managed.

Researching and setting up the logistical network to make this a viable venture took the better part of one and a half years. I had to develop a program that could be sold to pharmaceutical industry clients. We would be competing with well-established companies like Boron-Lepore. Where do I start?? First, I had to develop a system to support the moderators: airline travel, hotel reservations, rental car reservations, etc. Next, we had to develop a system to coordinate with the hotel or restaurant for meeting spaces and food. Next came the challenge of identifying physicians to invite to the meetings and a procedure to invite them. (The pharmaceutical industry client often had helpful suggestions.) Physicians attending these meetings were offered premiums that they could order from a prepared list of options. This obviously required identifying and qualifying a vendor that could handle these requests. Most important was the challenge of identifying and selecting high quality individuals for moderators. They would need training in the logistics of the job and, most importantly, training in the product/disease entity that they would be presenting. The moderator training would consist of the pharmaceutical industry client providing study materials to the moderator several weeks in advance of the program. It was critical that we hire very competent and reliable individuals who had the potential of becoming excellent moderators. Last but certainly not least, we had to develop a marketing effort to sell our services to potential industry clients. When we thought that we could start running programs, we had to have enough staff to ensure that all aspects of the meeting were covered. Initially, in addition to myself, we had two full-time employees assigned to the organization, as well as four part-time moderators.

The first program we ran was with Ivax Pharmaceuticals, which was headquartered in Miami, FL. I had to visit Ivax's top management in Miami to sell our services. We held peer influence meetings in four locations throughout the U.S. for the initial program. My old friend, Dave Bethune, was CEO of Ivax at the time. Did this help in getting Ivax to be the guinea pig for our first event? You bet!!! I had already selected moderators of the highest quality who had had significant experience with Boron-Lepore; I knew them personally. Even though the first session with Ivax exposed some rough edges we needed to work out, overall, due to the competent and experienced moderators, Sander, I and Ivax management considered the first Peer Perspectives dinner meetings to be successful.

In my previous discussions with Sander, I had agreed to a maximum of two years that I would commit to his organization. I had accomplished what Sander's goal was, and my two years were up. I left the Becker organization feeling good about what I was able to accomplish. "If you think you can, you can." Sander and I remained friends. Unfortunately, just as Peer Perspectives was about to get off the ground, the federal government began to discourage peer influence dinner meetings. They saw these meetings as an unethical method of promoting pharmaceutical products to physicians. Soon after, all these meetings were discontinued with pressure from the federal government. This effectively closed Peer Perspectives, Boron-Lepore, and several other companies who used this type of promotion. Peer Perspectives had a short life and never had the opportunity to become the force in the pharmaceutical market that it might have.

New Ventures

When we relocated from northern New Jersey several years earlier to get back to my first love, federal government sales, we had the perfect homestead. While it had been financially challenging early in my career to move from a low cost of living area in Chesapeake, VA, to a higher cost of living area in the Washington, D.C., metro area, we did it. Things got worse as we moved from the D.C. area to the NYC metro area, especially with mortgage interest rates at a high of 16%. Of course, I was pleased with each promotion, but my wife, Beverly, said "We are being promoted into poverty!" From a financial perspective, this often seemed to be true. As we moved back down south to northern VA, I was able to not only recover financially, but also to gain substantially in real estate transfers. With the sale of my house in Wyckoff, NJ, the bedroom community of NYC, I had a healthy amount of money to reinvest in Fairfax County, VA. We had the luxury of looking at the best the area had to offer. We eventually settled into a highly desirable, restricted community of five-acre lots. Our five-acre lot was a partially wooded compound including a beautiful 3,800 sq. ft. three-story house and tennis courts, all of which was enclosed by a rustic split-rail fence. To say we felt like we had arrived was an understatement, to say the least. All our neighbors were on five acres. Some had horses roaming on beautiful green pastures. Others focused on swimming pools, tennis courts, or other athletic pursuits, but all had large, elaborate homes. What a wonderful place to retire and just enjoy life; right?? I enjoyed life at Oak Glen, the name of our estate. I spent my time playing tennis with neighborhood partners, operating the riding lawnmower to keep our one-acre open space pristine, and just enjoying walking the property to seek out improvements. I, in fact, did make one major improvement in the property. While I have limited carpentry skills, I single-handedly built a gazebo overlooking the tennis court. ("If you think you can, you can!") Our children, Reid, Allison, and Stuart, as well as their friends, loved to come visit us and enjoy all Oak Glen had to offer.

During this period, I became reconnected with an old VA Tech classmate, T.O. Williams. T.O. was a retired Air Force Colonel who was working at VA Tech as a fundraiser. He was also instrumental in forming the VA

Tech Corps of Cadets Alumni Association. I became a member of the Board of Directors of this organization. Along with T.O. and others, our mission was to revive the Corps which was almost extinct with only 264 members. When T.O. and I had attended VA Tech (then VPI), all students were members of the Corps of Cadets except for veterans and girls. We were not about to let the Corps tradition at VA Tech die. We started raising scholarships and selling the benefits of the Corps to incoming students.

Today the Corps has a national reputation comparable to the military academies and numbers about 1,400. ("If you think you can, you can.") Students who are members of the Corps earn a minor in leadership in addition to their major area of study. Much of the credit for the Corps revitalization is based on the vision and early work of T.O. Williams, one of my very special friends.

Over time, Beverly and I decided to move further south and away from the Washington, D.C./Northern Virginia hectic pace. After all, we had spent about 15 years in this environment in five-year segments. We considered the Norfolk, VA, area, where we had previously lived. We looked seriously in the Williamsburg, VA, area, but ultimately settled in the Richmond, VA, area. We had a daughter and two young grandchildren who were motivators for that decision.

Life was good! We settled into a nice, quiet community in Midlothian, VA. As a couple, we became active in River Road United Methodist Church. We joined the Stonehenge Country Club where I settled into a regular golfing lifestyle. So much for the easy lifestyle: it seems there was a small organization in Richmond called Psychological Consultants, who performed services for pharmaceutical companies throughout the country. Specifically, they performed assessment and development services for these companies to help them determine the promotability of their employees; more about that later. Amazing as it seems, they had no one on staff with a history of pharmaceutical sales and management experience. Somehow, they discovered that a recently retired pharmaceutical executive was living in the area, and they felt someone with pharmaceutical experience might be helpful. As a result, I was able to start an interesting and enjoyable relationship with Psychological Consultants that lasted for about five years. I was considered a part-time, independent contractor.

Psychological Consultants' assessments were conducted in the Jefferson Hotel, a five-star hotel in Richmond, VA. The only exception to this was assessments for Purdue Frederick, the company that was later cited for improper marketing practices of opioid-based products. We traveled to their home office in New Haven, CT, to conduct assessment centers for their selected personnel. Typical candidates that companies sent to us for assessments were pharmaceutical sales representatives that were being considered for promotion to District Manager, or district mangers that were being considered for regional director positions. Evaluations were based on how the candidate handled simulated exercises that were typical of the job for which he or she was being considered. The simulated exercises were held over the course of about three days. Assessors would assign numerical evaluations for each action completed by the candidate. One day following the assessment center, assessors would meet and come to a group agreement on each candidate's performance. Following that, each assessor would write a report and a development plan for two candidates, which would be provided to the client company.

In addition to being an assessor, I often accompanied David Purdy, President of the company, on marketing trips. For these events, we would invite pharmaceutical companies to attend a seminar in which we educated them on the services we could provide. Later in my employment, I became the Vice-President of Sales and Marketing, devoting 100% of my time to increasing our client base. This period of my life was very rewarding. I became friends with fellow assessors and especially with David Purdy, the President. Our friendship lasts to this day.

Military Highlights

With thirty-three years total military service between U.S. Army active duty, Virginia Army National Guard, and U.S. Army Reserve, I would be remiss if I did not highlight some of my major assignments. This is particularly significant in that over fifteen years of my pharmaceutical career involved working directly with the U.S. military. My customers included Surgeon Generals of the Army, Navy, and Air Force, the U.S. Surgeon General, as well as U.S. military chiefs of medical service specialties, i.e., OB/GYN, Surgery, Urology, Dermatology, etc.; in addition, I made routine sales calls on the Defense Personnel Support Center Medical Division, Depot Systems, major U.S. and overseas medical centers, Commissary and Exchange headquarters, as well as Veterans' Administration headquarters. The unifying group that brought all these agencies together was The Association of Military Surgeons of the United States (AMSUS). To bypass the military/civilian interconnectivity for me would leave the story incomplete.

As stated earlier, I became intrigued with the military while I was still in high school. I joined a Virginia National Guard unit that was being formed in my town and served three years as an enlisted soldier. The unit was an anti-aircraft artillery battery. I had to resign from this unit when I accepted an advanced ROTC scholarship as a student in the Virginia Tech Corps of Cadets. Upon being commissioned as a 2nd Lieutenant in the U.S. Field Artillery, I attended the Field Artillery Officers' School at Fort Sill Oklahoma. Following that, I was assigned as a platoon leader in the Sixth Armored Calvary Regiment at Fort Knox Kentucky. Upon completing my active-duty tour, I was assigned to the 29th Infantry Division in Norfolk, VA. The 29th Division had made history as a lead unit in the Normandy Invasion on D-Day in World War II. In fact, the National D-Day Memorial in Bedford, VA, commemorates the loss of more soldiers from a single town than any other location in the country. These soldiers lost their lives as members of the 29th Division while participating in the Normandy invasion. I was selected to be the Aide-de-Camp to the commanding general of the 29th Infantry Division, General William C. Purnell. I held this assignment for about two years.

Following this assignment, I spent several years in the 111th Field Artillery Battalion, Virginia Army National Guard. My assignments in this unit included Battery Executive Officer, Battery Commander, and Battalion Liaison Officer. Much of our training with this unit occurred at Camp A.P. Hill, Virginia; Fort Pickett, Virginia; and Fort Indian Town Gap, Pennsylvania.

Just as in the civilian world, education is a continuing necessity for those who aspire to higher positions. During much of my military career, I was involved with the United States Army Reserve (USAR) school system as a student and/or instructor. I completed the Officer

Advance Course, the Army Command and General Staff College, and part of the Air War College through the USAR school system. The classes were conducted locally as well as onsite during summer training periods at Fort Sill, Oklahoma, and Fort Leavenworth, Kansas.

My first assignment in the U.S. Army Reserve was Commandant of the First U.S. Army NCO Academy, Fort Meade, Maryland. By now I had completed the Army Command and General Staff College. I discovered that I enjoyed teaching, so I elected to attend the Command and General Staff Instructor School, which included a two-week assignment onsite at Fort Leavenworth, Kansas. I spent much of my reserve service time as a Command and General Staff College instructor. This provided a great deal of flexibility as I operated independently and could schedule my classes so as not to interfere with my civilian work. I could select the time I taught, as well as the location. I have taught in many locations in the Washington, D.C., area, including The Pentagon, Fort Belvoir, Fort McNair, and other Department of Defense facilities. My students were regular Army officers or Reserve officers who chose this method rather than attending the resident course at Fort Leavenworth, Kansas. One of the most unusual teaching locations I had was the Westchester County Airport in New York. Most of my students at this location were Army Reserve officers who were airline pilots in their civilian careers.

After several years of teaching and approaching burnout, I was assigned as a military academy liaison officer for West Point, essentially a field admissions representative. This assignment also had the flexibility to perform independently. West Point would provide me with the names of high-potential applicants. I, in turn, interviewed the applicants at a mutually convenient time and provided my recommendations to West Point Admissions. This process debunks the misinformation that the critical element for admissions was knowing a congressman. In most cases, the congressman nominated those applicants that were recommended to them by West Point.

These several years of working with West Point as a military academy liaison officer was a lead to my last U.S. Army assignment. During the time that I was serving as a military academy liaison officer, I was also attending the U.S. Army Inspector General School. I was appointed by Department of the Army to be the West Point Inspector General IMA. IMA stands for "Individual Mobilization Augmentee". In other words, if for any reason the full-time Inspector General was not able to serve, I would be activated to take his place. To perform my duty, I spent my active-duty assignments at West Point performing IG duties.

I enjoyed this assignment very much and served in that capacity for five years. I worked directly for the Superintendent of West Point, a 3-star-general. The IG performs two basic functions: first, inspect, i.e., identify problems, and, if present, make suggestions for correction; second, the IG is a source for soldiers/cadets to consult with in confidence if they feel their chain of command is not working well. I worked for two different superintendents during my tenure. Both generals valued my services, respected my opinions, and gave me the authority and support I needed to do the job. Importantly to me, they gave me among the best officer evaluation reports that I received in my entire Army career.

All good things must come to an end. To top off my Army career, Department of the Army submitted my name to be Deputy Commander, 97th Army Reserve Command. This is a Brigadier General slot! I was not selected, but I had a good run!! I retired.

Life As a Politician

During the time I was working with Psychological Consultants, I became active in the local Republican Party. Eventually, I became Chairman of the Midlothian District Precinct. I enjoyed working with local politicians and citizen activists. In the process, I developed many friendships and contacts with the Chesterfield County Republican Committee. When a vacancy was about to occur on the Chesterfield County Board of Supervisors, I was encouraged to become a candidate for that position. My first reaction was totally negative to the idea, but with much show of support from many friends, I decided to give it a shot. The first step was running in the Republican Primary. Even as a novice in politics, I easily won the Republican Primary over three other candidates. Now the business of politics became very real, for sure. Chesterfield County at the time was the third largest county in the State of Virginia, with a population of 325,000. The Midlothian District, for which I was attempting to fill the role of Supervisor, had a population of 65,000 residents; it was one of five districts in Chesterfield County. The five Supervisors of these districts were the governing body of the county. As Chesterfield County is the bedroom community of Richmond, VA, the state capital, the Supervisors of Chesterfield have significant interaction with the governing body of the State of Virginia.

I quickly learned that running for public office, while exciting, was also very challenging. It's not a venture for the faint of heart. After completing all the necessary paperwork with the county for my candidacy, I learned who my Democratic opponent would be. His name was Dan Gecker, a Princeton-educated lawyer, who was currently serving on the Planning Commission for the Supervisor that was vacating the slot. He would prove to be a formidable opponent. My work was cut out for me; where do I start? I would need to select a Campaign Manager and a Campaign Treasurer, both of which were paid positions. I would need a cadre of reliable volunteers to campaign door-to-door for me, put up signs, pass out flyers, etc. Based on advice from political operatives who had been active in many previous campaigns, I learned that I would need to raise campaign funds or spend my own money. This is a part of campaigning that I dislike, but it is necessary. There would be costs for signs, campaign flyers, salaries for campaign staff, radio and newspaper ads, etc. Raising funds falls to the candidate rather than the staff. As previously stated, while fundraising was the least desirable part of my campaigning, I raised in excess of $100,000 in about three months. Donations ranged from $5 to $10,000, with most donations in the $50-$75 range. Election laws require periodic reporting of funds raised by candidates. Normally these donations are published in the local newspaper. Developers who want to engage the favor of Supervisors tend to be in the larger contribution category. While developers are a good source for funds, this can be a liability for the candidate if the public perceives that a less-than-professional relationship exists between the developer and the candidate. During this timeframe, Chesterfield was in a rapid residential growth phase. Many residents wanted to keep the quiet, rural nature of the area and were anti-growth. I would later be accused of catering to developers based on my vote of approval of several new zoning requests.

As my campaign got into the active mode, my life was consumed with introducing myself to citizens and asking for their vote; campaign meetings with paid staff and volunteers; speaking to local groups, clubs, community associations, etc. I spent many days handing out literature at shopping centers in addition to walking neighborhoods and knocking on doors. I learned somewhat the hard way that passing out literature at shopping center parking lots was less productive than calling on individual homes. Much of the effort at shopping centers was wasted because I had no way of knowing whether individuals were Democrat or Republican, whether they lived in my district, and whether they were likely voters. One of my volunteer supporters, Marie Quinn, was a seasoned political operative who was a major force in the Republican Party of Virginia and who also had significant involvement at the national level. She convinced me of the importance of door-to-door calling on known Republicans and known voters. She was able to provide me specific information on the party and voter status by individual home addresses. It took some convincing from her, but Marie was right – it's not the amount of literature you pass out or the number of people you contact. It's about targeting efforts toward those who actually vote, who are likely Republican voters, and who vote in your district. Among other parts of the busy campaigning schedule, I participated in two debates with my opponent, Dan Gecker. The major debate was organized by the Chamber of Commerce. The results of these debates were published in several newspapers and excerpts on radio stations. I felt I held my own in these debates.

I attribute much of my ultimate success as a novice politician to Marie Quinn. In the process, I got to know and become friends with the then current Governor, Bob McDonald. I developed a very special friendship with former Governor and Senator George Allen. In addition, I developed a relationship with former Governor Jim Gilmore. Both Governor Allen and Governor Gilmore were very active in local Republican politics in the Richmond area. They both made speeches in my behalf on several occasions at Republican events. Governor Allen was a guest for an event at my home in Midlothian. My wife and I were frequent guests in Governor Gilmore's home for his annual Christmas party. I had easy access to Senator Allen's D.C. office on Capitol Hill when he was in that role. I attribute a significant amount of my success as a local politician to my relationships with and the efforts of Governor Allen and Governor Gilmore. I would be remiss if I did not also give credit to then State Senator John Watkins, who supported me in numerous ways. Much of the work and success of my campaign was conducted by a group of volunteers that are too numerous to mention by name.

Finally, the campaign was over and election day had arrived. I spent that day visiting as many polling places as possible (approximately 15 in the district) greeting voters, asking for their support, and thanking my volunteer supporters who were passing out literature. My opponent, Dan Gecker, had a volunteer staff doing the same thing. Most of the campaigning at the polling places was very low-key and soft sell. Election laws are very specific and selective on activities that can take place at the polling place. At the end of the day, I emerged as the winner by a significant margin. I was, of course, elated but also somewhat overwhelmed by the new responsibility. That night I met with a huge crowd of supporters at the Richmond Convention Center where I gave my acceptance speech and thanked the exuberant crowd for their support. On the next day, a first occurred for me! My picture was on the front page of The Richmond Times Dispatch. I was being congratulated with a big hug from a supporter. The story of my victory consumed the entire front page of the paper. During the campaign, while I had always had some concerns about whether I would win, the overriding emotion that I experienced was that I would emerge victorious. ("If you think you can, you can.")

After being sworn in and undergoing an extensive orientation, my work as a supervisor began. The Board of Supervisors typically meets once a month in the evening at the county administrative buildings. Occasionally, special meetings are called. Except for some meetings that are closed to the public based on the nature of the discussions, all meetings are opened to the public. Our typical meetings had 100-200 attendees. This is the time that developers presented zoning cases for approval, business owners requested licenses or changes in their operations, and the Board of Supervisors reviewed any citizen issues that were on the agenda for consideration. After the official meeting was complete, citizens who had signed up could speak, normally limited to three minutes each, on issues of their choosing. Typically, meetings lasted about three hours; however, I have participated in meetings that lasted from 7:00 p.m. to 2:00 a.m. Termination of the meetings during early morning hours was not unusual.

The role of Supervisor is extensive and varied. Some Supervisors maintain full-time jobs, relying on assistants in the county office to handle many of the required tasks. In my case, I devoted full time to carrying out the duties of my position. Duties included establishing the county budget; establishing the county tax rate; appointing individuals to commissions; supervising county administration; participating in regional government associations; and taking care of district business. During my tenure, we also hired a new county administrator.

A typical day for me consisted of answering as many as 20 phone calls per day; meeting with constituents and addressing their issues; and frequently attending meetings of county organizations. Often, I was invited as a speaker for civic associations. On most evenings, I had to decide which, if any, invitations to community civic association meetings I would accept.

During my tenure on the Board, the two most significant accomplishments in which I was a prime mover included redevelopment of the Cloverleaf Mall and the development of the Watkins Center. The Cloverleaf Mall was an older mall that over time had shown signs of aging and deterioration and was losing customers. The Watkins Center, on the other hand, was a proposed new development in the suburbs which promised state-of-the-art facilities. While these activities had supporters, they also had a significant number of opponents. Both activities were in my district; however, the entire county would be the source of funding, which would be a major expenditure for the county. Shepherding these projects and gaining support for them consumed the bulk of my time. In the end, both were approved. Cloverleaf Mall today is once again a thriving shopping mall, residential and office community. The Watkins Center is an ultramodern assortment of shopping, restaurants, and entertainment venues, as well as light office and residential buildings. Both centers are destinations for the entire Richmond, VA, region.

While I feel good about most decisions I made during my term as Supervisor, one bad decision I made fostered my loss in the next election. In Chesterfield County, VA, the Supervisor appoints his or her selection of Planning Commissioner for the district. The Planning

Commissioner holds a powerful position and interacts with the public to make recommendations to the Supervisor. In a desirable arrangement, there exists a strong and trusting relationship between the Supervisor and the Planning Commissioner. The Planning Commissioner for the Midlothian District, Dan Gecker, was previously appointed by the Democratic Supervisor I was replacing. This Supervisor was forced to resign based on inappropriate actions with a female county staffer. Dan approached me and requested that he continue to serve as my Planning Commissioner. He was a well-qualified, Princeton-trained lawyer, and had served competently in the position. While he was of the opposite political party, I agreed to keep him on as my Planning Commissioner. This was a serious political blunder for me. It turns out that unknown to me at the time, he had plans to run against me in the next election. So much for me trying to be a nice guy rather than trying to make the right political decision. From day one, rather than being my trusted advisor, he worked behind the scenes to discredit my positions, and in fact, started his own campaign for my position. Virginia law states that a Planning Commissioner cannot be terminated involuntarily until the term of the Supervisor who appointed him comes to an end. I blew it!!! While I enjoyed my role as a major political figure in Virginia politics, I was somewhat relieved when my term was over. I lost the upcoming election to Dan Gecker.

Fifty Years With Beverly, the Love of My Life

It so happened that one of the rare days that Dad let me drive his car to school became a very important day for me! During the lunch period, Beverly spilled an entire glass of chocolate milk on her always tastefully selected dress. She was a mess!! While I did not know her well at that time, I had had my eye on her exceptional good looks and her quiet but pleasing personality. An immediate opportunity was apparent to me. "Can I take you home so you can change your dress?" I asked. She lived in town, so this was a reasonable solution. She replied in a somewhat relieved voice, "Yes, I would appreciate it." Wow! My lucky day to have had access to a car. That unexpected and unlikely event was the start of a three-year dating period and fifty-plus years of marriage: an event that has had a positive impact in my life to this day.

Early on, we fell madly in love, spending every possible minute with each other. Many felt we were an uneven match, with Beverly being the cultured city girl, and me the country hick farm boy. Fortunately, she saw possibilities in me. Beverly encouraged me to run for Student Body President at Franklin County High School. At first, I was reluctant, but one night in a quiet moment looking up into the stars during my prayer time, I felt the Lord was telling me to go for it. She was my successful campaign manager and provided me the opportunity to serve in the first of many leadership roles. ("If you think you can, you can.") After high school, we each headed off to different colleges – Beverly to Mary Washington University and I to Virginia Tech. After a year at Mary Washington, with infrequent time with each other, Beverly returned to Roanoke to continue her education at National Business College. We started talking the impractical, but inevitable plans for our marriage. In the spring of my junior year, we tied the knot. Our plan – Beverly would work while I finished school. A great plan we thought! The unplanned arrival of Reid, our first son, changed the plan dramatically. I still had a year of college to complete, as well as a wife and son who relied on me for support. I worked every other night at the Sealtest condensery in Christiansburg. The income from that job, plus a $27.50 ROTC monthly check, kept us afloat. These were very lean times but looking back – some of the happiest times of our lives. We lived in town with other struggling young couples. We had our own social network, with some of the individuals becoming lifelong friends.

It was great to start receiving a check in the amount of $222/month when I entered the U.S. Army as a Second Lieutenant. Beverly and I enjoyed our time together on active duty, with duty stations at Fort Sill, OK, and Fort Knox, KY. After active duty, I remained in the Virginia National Guard and U.S. Army Reserve for a total of 33 years of service. Beverly was very supportive of my weekend and weeknight drills, and infrequent call-ups for short active-duty tours. She never complained and enjoyed the additional income throughout my career. She told her friends that while their husbands were out playing golf on weekends, her husband was out playing soldier.

Our first permanent location was in Norfolk, VA, initially with Sealtest Foods, and later with Lederle Laboratories. The early years of Reid, Allison and Stuart were all spent in Norfolk, VA. We developed a special family friendship with Ann and Les Miller, who had three children, Les, Lori, and David, who were the corresponding ages of our children. Ann and Beverly packed all six kids in the back of my Renault and spent most every day at the beach. This friendship has lasted to this day.

In time, I was promoted to District Manager for Lederle in the Washington, D.C., area. Beverly's assessment was that we were being promoted into poverty. The $14,000 which I was able to sell our brick bungalow for in Norfolk didn't go very far in finding a suitable replacement home in Fairfax, VA.

Nevertheless, we enjoyed what would be the first of three times we would be assigned to the area. We developed lifelong friends while we were in the D.C. area. Most notable were the VanWagoner's, with whom we spent many happy hours. Both Beverly and I were pleased that Reid, Allison, and Stuart had the benefit of being educated in what is arguably some of the best schools in America. A part of their education was being in the middle of where our nation's rules were being made. Just as important, we were living among the people that were making it happen. Beverly was especially supportive of my work during this period. District Managers were not provided secretaries, although an abundance of oral and written communication was required. Beverly performed all these secretarial duties without pay and maintained a positive and cheerful attitude throughout.

Our first experience in the corporate headquarters life occurred after five years in the D.C. area. We were off to northern New Jersey, just across the Hudson River from New York City. Again, housing was even more expensive there than in the D.C. area. While I was pleased with the promotion, I was beginning to appreciate Beverly's analysis of the situation: "being promoted into poverty." Despite the generous increase in pay, it just did not seem to make up for the significant increase in housing costs and cost of living.

This was the first for all of us as Southerners to adapt to Yankee ways and lingo. Particularly, Beverly, with her charming southern accent, had challenges. When you've said, "How are y'all?" for 35 years, it's hard to change. This was one of our most challenging assignments. The kids had to meet all new friends, our next-door neighbor was less than welcoming, my job was very demanding – consuming 60-80 hours per week. This left all the child-raising and household issues to Beverly. She handled it like a real trouper and without complaining. We survived this assignment, as we knew it was temporary and a necessary part of the long-term growth pattern.

We were headed back to the D.C. area after two years and now our living costs were down in comparison to the New York City area. We settled into a comfortable lifestyle in the same neighborhood that we had left; and with many of our old friends. The children were now older and required less of Beverly's attention. She was able to relax a bit now and enjoy life more. Also, my new job, while challenging, was less stressful.

After a time, the call to corporate life came again in the New York City metro area. This time, however, I was higher in the corporate structure. This job presented a new set of opportunities and challenges. We had to learn the politics of corporate life. This was a particular challenge for Beverly. The wives' social status was directly tied to the husband's position in the company. Neither she nor I was fine-tuned into corporate politics, and in fact, we detested it. I was high up enough in the organization to not be intimidated. The great benefit to Beverly was that she was able to travel with me on many company trips. During this assignment, we visited many of the finest resorts in the country, and in fact, the world; this was at company expense for first class service. Our trips included places like The Doral in Florida, Hotel Del Coronado in San Diego, as well as most well-known resorts in the U.S. Additionally, we visited resorts in Hawaii, Nevis, Mexico, and others. Beverly enjoyed these trips which were social for the wives. In these settings, corporate protocol was downplayed.

During these years, our kids were in college, so this reduced our parenting requirements. We developed a great relationship with Billie and Al Stubmann of Franklin Lakes, NJ. Beverly planned a wedding for the marriage of our daughter, Allison, to Paul White while we were serving in the New Jersey corporate headquarters. Not to minimize the challenges, the wedding and reception were to be held in Rocky Mount, VA, in the same church where Beverly and I were married, and Beverly had considerable help from her sister, Eleanor, who was living not far away in Smith Mountain Lake, VA. The reception was to be held at the Waterfront Country Club at Smith Mountain Lake. Beverly did not miss a trick. Even though the wedding was four states away from us, it came off without a hitch. This is a good example of Beverly's resourcefulness and attention to detail.

As I was nearing retirement, we elected to move back to Northern Virginia. Having been stressed financially in our moves north, we received the benefit as we moved back south. We bought a five-acre estate in Fairfax County, VA, Oak Glen, complete with split-rail fence and tennis court. The house, a three-level structure, had a complete set of living quarters on the lower level. While we were there, we had a young female divorcee, Barbara

Marshall, who occupied this space. She became a second daughter to us. Later, our son, Reid, who had undergone a serious neurological event, and his family lived in the space for about a year. Reid had a temporary disability and was unable to work for many months. We enjoyed this location as one of our very favorites for several years. I was semi-retired and doing part-time consulting work. Beverly and I were able to enjoy the beauty of the estate, and we also had more time for each other.

In time, we decided to move closer to our roots and family members. Allison and Paul lived in Richmond with their two children at that time. We eventually ended up in that area. Being semi-retired gave me the opportunity to become involved in politics. While Beverly was not politically motivated, she was very supportive of my efforts. We enjoyed this period of our lives with time being devoted to church, grandchildren, politics, and our beach house in Corolla, NC.

Life was very good to us in those days. Eventually, Beverly started having back pains that were unexplained. She visited her family physician, and at his recommendation, she participated in physical therapy for a brief period. With no apparent improvement, she started visits to various specialists, but to no avail. Ultimately, her family physician suggested she be tested for pancreatic cancer. This resulted in her diagnosis as confirmed pancreatic cancer, and in her being referred to an oncologist. The next few months became a very difficult time. Beverly's pain, reduced strength, and lack of appetite were increasing daily. My efforts as her caregiver were the best I could muster, but still inadequate. My most significant challenge was trying to find and prepare something she could eat. Toward the end, the only thing she could ingest was a few sips of Ensure daily.

Beverly was always a very private person. She did not want anyone to know of her condition. Of course, the children were aware, and all had their private conversations with her. The only people outside of the family that she desired to have contact with were Emily Moore, the Associate Pastor at our church, River Road United Methodist Church, and Mary Erickson, Director of Music/Organist. She had a special relationship with each of them.

Since we were not satisfied with Beverly's oncologist, we decided as a family that a change was necessary. Our son, Stuart, and his employees had connections with the best oncologists and treatment centers in the country. After Stuart's investigation, we decided to admit Beverly to the Lombardy Cancer Center at Georgetown University in Washington, D.C., for treatment. On the day of her admission, as was her daily custom, Beverly dressed impeccably 'to the nines' despite her weakened condition. Stuart, Allison, and I accompanied Beverly for the trip to Georgetown University Hospital. We were all present for her preadmission examination. While being examined on the examination table, she suddenly fell back; that was the end!! None of us had the chance to say "goodbye." She was immediately moved to the trauma center, but despite heroic efforts by the center's best to revive her, it failed. After an hour of hoping, agonizing, and praying with mixed emotions, Allison, Stuart, and I were informed of her passing. That was the start of a major, lasting void, but fond memories that would last over my lifetime.

New Beginnings

Only those who have lost a spouse can identify with the grief, despair, and aloneness that one experiences in this situation. I was a perfect example of this scenario. Despite neighbors adopting me for meals, as well as church and family members coming to my aid for support, my life was incomplete. I had no interest in other women, yet I was an unhappy camper. I looked for ways and events to fill the void, much of it related to church activities. On a mission trip with River Road United Methodist Church, I had a long drive to far southwest Virginia with my friend, Bill Graeter. During our lengthy discussion, the idea of getting on with my new life consumed much of our three-hour trip.

When we first moved to Richmond, VA, Beverly and I became very much involved with River Road United Methodist Church. In time, I became a member of the choir, and both Beverly and I were involved in multiple church activities. At one time, I served as Chairman of the Board of Trustees. I was also on the Staff-Parish Relations Committee. Both Beverly and I very much admired the then Director of Music/Organist, Mary Erickson, from our early experience at the church. Each member of the Staff-Parish Relations Committee was assigned a specific staff person to mentor and to be a liaison person to the congregation. My assignment was Mary Erickson. I enjoyed a good professional relationship with her in that capacity for several years.

Back to my conversation with my friend, Bill Graeter, on starting a new life; he asked me: "Have you ever thought about Mary Erickson?" Frankly, at the time, I had not considered any female for future companionship. Out of the blue, a light went on in my head. I credit Bill with giving me the idea to stop feeling sorry for myself and the possibility of starting a new life. A natural new possibility was opened to me from that conversation. Afterall, I had known Mary for several years, and we had been casual friends during that time. She had also been a casual friend of Beverly's for several years. In fact, as previously mentioned, Mary was one of only two people Beverly had requested to have contact with before her passing. I later learned from Mary that a significant part of that conversation was Beverly expressing a concern for my well-being. Was that a God-motivated meeting?

"God works in mysterious ways His wonders to perform."

At any rate, Mary and I did start a relationship that led to our marriage. Mary gave me a new lease on life, and has been my best friend, wife, and trusted companion for the last several years. She has moved with me from Richmond, VA, to The Outer Banks of North Carolina, and most recently to Roanoke, VA. She has been and is my rock in difficult times, and my hope and joy in good times. I tell all who are interested in listening that God has provided me with two wonderful wives. Both have supported and support me well beyond what I deserve. I shudder to think what would have happened to me if Mary had not become an integral part of my life. I thank the Lord every day for my life and the fact that each of my wives have made it whole. God did not create man to live alone; especially true for men like me who need that occasional nudge or encouragement from someone who shares their life's goals. "If you think you can, you can."

The Moving Bug Hits Again

During the early 70's, I purchased a lot in Corolla, NC. It was an undeveloped piece of oceanfront property. During the next several years, the area developed by leaps and bounds becoming one of the premiere vacation destinations in the eastern U.S. and indeed many parts of the world. The property was in the northern part of the famous Outer Banks of North Carolina, which includes places like Nags Head, Kitty Hawk, Manteo, Southern Shores, and Duck. When I bought the property, the only access to the area was over sand with a four-wheel-drive vehicle. The famous Corolla wild horses, which were later moved further north to Carova, were roaming over the property.

In 1988 at the start of the boom, I built a vacation rental house on the property. My family and I enjoyed the property as a vacation home for many years. We gathered each summer while my grandchildren grew from infants to teenagers and beyond. Beverly and I, plus Reid and Cheryl, Allison and Paul, and Stuart and Rusty, as well as all the grandchildren, gathered there for the week of July 4th and longer, when possible, for some of the best and most memorable times of our lives. It was a comfortable five-bedroom house just off the ocean. At the time, a five-bedroom house was a big house for the area. Now much larger multi-million-dollar homes are the standard. As our grandchildren grew up with their own lives and job changes, this took the family in many different directions. Our memorable family gatherings thus faded away. I continued to maintain the property as a vacation rental investment.

After Mary and I had lived together in Richmond for a couple of years, we started discussing the idea of moving to Corolla as our permanent place of residence. We did in fact, after much consideration, decide to make the move to the Corolla property. Initially, we maintained our Richmond home as well and made frequent trips between the two locations.

Our home in Corolla introduced us to a new and exciting adventure. We very much enjoyed the walks on the beach, the beautiful evening sunsets over the Currituck Sound, and sunrises over the ocean. Particularly pleasant was listening to the crashing waves and enjoying cool ocean breezes with open windows. Spring and Fall were our favorite times of the year. The busy summer vacationers were gone, and we could enjoy the solitude of the area along with the few other permanent residents.

Our property was in Section E of Ocean Sands across Highway 12 from the Currituck Golf and Country Club. Our only nearby neighbors were Bill and Dyan Crone, who lived across the street. We became very special friends with them. In the wintertime, November thru March, Corolla was very sparsely populated. Most restaurants closed. The local Food Lion and Harris Teeter remained open, but with limited options, especially of fresh produce. For any major shopping, we drove south for about 20 miles to more populated Southern Shores.

During this time, I was working for the Corolla Wild Horse Fund. We were the group that managed the famous Spanish mustangs that were brought to America hundreds of years earlier by Spanish explorers. They were either thrown overboard just offshore during stormy conditions, or they survived shipwrecks and swam ashore. At any rate, they survived and became natural inhabitants of The Outer Banks and depended on natural grasses, leaves, vines, or whatever they could find to eat for subsistence. To this day, they eat only items that grow naturally in the sandy, windswept environment. Their digestive systems have adapted to this food source, and they receive no supplemental food from man. In fact, tourists are forbidden to feed the horses and are subject to severe fines if they attempt to do so. The reason for this is twofold. Apples or other foods that are not a part of their natural diet can cause constipation or death, especially for young animals. Also, the plan is to keep the horses wild and to prevent their domestication. In addition, tourists are prohibited from getting within 50 feet of the horses with again the potential for severe fines. The tourist rules are for their safety. The horses are wild, consequently, very unpredictable. They fight frequently and pose an unsuspecting threat to tourists who do not respect the rules. My role with the Corolla Wild Horse Fund was serving as a sanctuary patrol officer. In that role, I protected the horses from invasion by tourists. Even though the rules were posted and well-understood, some tourists insisted on trying to feed the horses or getting close enough to pet them. They totally ignored their own safety or the damage they could inflict on the horses by feeding them or getting too close. Most tourists responded to verbal reminders of the rules, but occasionally some were less cooperative. At times, this required engaging the sheriff's department for assistance in resolving the issue.

The other part of my role was taking tourists on tours to see the horses. This was a most enjoyable part of the job. I typically gave my tour group about a ten-minute briefing on the history of the horses. I then loaded the passengers into a four-wheel-drive Suburban SUV for the approximately two-hour tour. We, of course, would be driving along the beach in soft sand, and even though we lowered the tire pressure to about 13 lbs., we were still subject to getting stuck. Driving on soft sand along the beach presents a challenge for even the most experienced driver. The beach was frequently inundated with vehicles stuck in the sand. Experienced drivers knew to keep up their speed and to avoid stuck vehicles. In approximately seven years of driving, I was stuck only once with a load of passengers. The good news for those who got stuck was that wreckers were plentiful along the beach which would pull them out for a fee. The fee was typically one hundred dollars to three hundred dollars, depending on how badly you were stuck or how eager you were to get pulled out. The secret was to negotiate with the wrecker driver.

The horses were occasionally on the beach splashing in the surf to cool off. More frequently they were behind the dune line, which required crossing over the dunes to search them out. Many times, it was difficult to find horses, as they tended to move back to the marshes on the back side of the island and the Currituck Sound. The horses live and move in harems of two to ten or more horses. Every harem has at least one stallion; the dominant stallion had several mares (females) in his harem. The stallions that were the best fighters had the most mares in their harem. In other words, the way a stallion populates his harem with mares is to fight an opposing stallion to get his mares. After several years of touring, I learned the most likely places that I would find horses. On most tours, I was able to locate from one up to several harems. In the cool of winter season, horses moved back into the forested and brushy areas, making them much harder to find. It was not uncommon to find only one harem, or sometimes just one horse. ("If you think you can, you can.") Tour passengers were always happy if I was able to find only one horse; however, the more I found the more excited they became. Bottom line, most of the excitement was generated by the hunt itself. I can truthfully say that the most fun I had in a job was working with the Corolla Wild Horse Fund.

As I pointed out previously, during the late fall and winter months, when the tourists are gone, things get pretty quiet and lonesome up in Corolla. With Mary's job down south at The Outer Banks Welcome Center in Kitty Hawk and with most of our activities including church, shopping, and friends being down south in the

Duck/Southern Shores areas, we started discussing the possibility of a move in that direction. We ultimately did buy a place and moved to Southern Shores across from The Duck Woods Country Club. This proved to be a very good move for us.

Life in Southern Shores

Southern Shores is a small town located between Kitty Hawk, NC, and Duck, NC. The town is populated, for the most part, by full-time residents. This provided a more complete feeling of community than Corolla, which was very sparsely populated from October to March and was inundated with tourists from June to September.

We found a small but very nice house in a managed community called Mallard Cove. The exterior of the house and all community lawn and shrubbery were taken care of by the HOA. This appealed to us and had a positive impact on our decision to buy in this community. The location worked very well for us. While we were not on the oceanfront now, we had a large lake behind our property, and we were able to enjoy water views from a screened-in back porch.

Mary was only a five-minute drive to the visitor center where she worked. While I had a thirty-minute drive to the Corolla Wild Horse Fund, it was a most beautiful drive along the Currituck Sound. We had just bought a convertible automobile, and my drive along the sound watching the marvelous sunsets with cool ocean breezes was unforgettable.

Mary and I were both very active in the Duck United Methodist Church music program. I sang bass in the choir, and she assisted the music director by playing the piano for the choir and substituting on the organ occasionally. Later, we became involved in The Outer Banks Chorus, a group comprised of community singers from throughout The Outer Banks and beyond. The director and accompanist were paid professionals. The Outer Banks Chorus developed a regional reputation and performed at least two concerts annually that drew audiences from as far away as tidewater Virginia and central North Carolina. In addition to singing in the chorus, Mary served on the Board and assisted with accompanying as needed. Her musical involvement in the community also included being a board member for the Eastern Carolina Concert Society and substituting as organist/pianist at churches from Nags Head to Corolla. My involvement in these musical pursuits continued alongside my organizing the bluegrass band I named Seagrass; more on this later.

A major social group in Southern Shores is the Southern Shores Boat Club. Dare County, which includes the towns of Manteo, Nags Head, Kill Devil Hills, Kitty Hawk, and Southern Shores, is covered by 60% water. This is in addition to the Atlantic Ocean, which borders the County. It goes without saying that a town with rivers, sounds, canals, tributaries, and lakes would have a fair number of boaters. The Southern Shores Boat Club owns and maintains two marinas where local boat owners dock their boats. The largest marina has a large, covered pavilion where social events are held. The pavilion is conveniently located on a beautiful piece of land at one of the major boat entrances to the sound. Most members of the boat club are current or prior boat owners. Due to age and other factors, the club has evolved into more of a social club rather than a boater's club. During our stay in The Outer Banks, Mary and I became members of The Southern Shores Boat Club.

One of the most appealing aspects of the club is a monthly breakfast meeting at the Duck Woods Country Club. In addition to a great breakfast, we had a chance to reconnect and socialize with friends. Also, we had a distinguished speaker of note at each meeting. My task was to arrange for speakers, which I did for about two years. In addition to these breakfast meetings, we had several functions at the pavilion which I assisted in planning. Most notable were the Independence Day celebration and the Christmas Boat Parade. I suppose I did OK in these roles, as eventually I was nominated to become Commodore of the Boat Club. This was more responsibility than I wanted, but nevertheless, I was elected to the position of Commodore, Southern Shores Boat Club, a position I held until just before leaving The Outer Banks. ("If you think you can, you can"). The Boat

Club was a quasi-political organization. The Mayor of Southern Shores, Tom Bennett, one of my best friends, was a former Commodore of the Boat Club. The Boat Club had a significant voice in local town politics. The Commodore position was demanding and required a considerable amount of my time. Despite that, I enjoyed the role very much. Because of my leadership with the Boat Club, I met and became friends with many Southern Shores residents that I would not have been exposed to otherwise. During the time we lived in Southern Shores, I was appointed to the Planning Commission. This gave me exposure to a different group of people and provided me the opportunity to have an impact on local government.

We developed many special friends while living in The Outer Banks; one of them was Diana Johnson, a widow. T.O. Williams, my VA Tech classmate and a best friend, who had lost his wife a couple of years earlier, was visiting us from Blacksburg, VA. We invited Diana to join us for dinner to make a foursome for board games. Diana and T.O. became instant friends and later companions. Diana and T.O. spent many happy hours together, and on numerous occasions Mary and I joined them for dinner at our place or Diana's. Their new relationship created many months of happiness for both until T.O.'s untimely and unexpected passing. This was, of course, a sad time for Diana. It was an especially sad time for me, as this was the first time that I had experienced the loss of one who had been a lifetime friend. I was honored to speak at his funeral, but it was a challenge.

For much of the time we lived in The Outer Banks we also maintained a home in Richmond, VA. We would frequently travel to Richmond and spend a week there. Over time, it became a bit tiring and challenging to maintain two houses. As a result, we decided to sell the Richmond house. Our Richmond house held most of our valuable furniture, family heirlooms, etc., which would not fit into our Mallard Cove Home. We, at the same time, had become intrigued with a beautiful, large home across the lake from our place in Mallard Cove. The house, sitting high on a hill, overlooked the Currituck Sound to the front and the lake on the backside. The property included about four acres. While much of this was marshland, it afforded a great water view from both the front and back. We enjoyed seeing the wide variety of boats that navigated the sound.

We decided to purchase this house due in part to wanting a place for our Richmond furniture. The move from Mallard Cove to Ginguite Trail was somewhat easier than previous moves as we could take small items in the car just around the lake. After the relocation of our Richmond furniture, as well as some from Mallard Cove, we enjoyed living in this home very much. It's hard to beat watching ducks and migratory birds splashing in the lake as we enjoyed cool evening breezes on our deck.

The property was heavily treed. Equally exhilarating was watching sunsets over the sound with a sailboat in view while swinging on our wrap-around front porch. We did not sell the Mallard Cove property; we rented it to long-term tenants. We could easily keep up with their activities as we could see them just across the lake.

Mary and I both enjoyed living in our new place on Ginguite Trail in Southern Shores very much. Our lives were very full as we were engaged in so many activities throughout The Outer Banks. For me carrying out the duties as Commodore of the Southern Shores Boat Club and fulfilling my responsibilities on the Planning Commission, while working with the Corolla Wild Horse Fund, kept me well-occupied. Somehow, I still found time to organize the bluegrass band which I named Seagrass. We rehearsed one night a week and sometimes had performances the same week.

To say the least, we had a very busy, but rewarding life. Most importantly, we got to know and spend relaxing time with many friends who remain dear to us today. Among the friends with whom we still maintain contact are Gary and Taunya Moore, Diana Johnson, Tom and Jayne Bennett, Michael and Nancy Terry, and George and Karon Grinnan. While I have enjoyed every place I have lived in my lifetime, I would have to say that living in Southern Shores, NC, was one of the best. While The Outer Banks, including Corolla and Southern Shores, are subject to hurricanes, in our 8+ years living there, we never had to evacuate. We did, however, experience several times when warnings and preparation were very real.

On the Road Again

As stated previously, our home in Southern Shores sat high upon a hill. This was great for views, but more importantly, we did not have to worry about flooding, which is a major issue in some parts of The Outer Banks. Our beautifully landscaped property required a significant amount of effort to keep it looking nice. A lot of hand-cutting and mowing was required on the backside of the house. While we had upstairs rooms in the house, we lived mostly on the first-floor level. One thing I was starting to notice was the climb up the hill from the mailbox and the stairs into the house, as well as the seemingly continuous work to keep the property up. Suddenly it hit me – why should I be surprised? I'm 83 years old!! Not only that, but I had also just completed a lengthy treatment for prostate cancer. Bottom line, it was time to start thinking about downsizing. Wow! That brought up a whole new set of decision-making we had not experienced before. After having lived in many different places in the country, where would we settle? What were we looking for in what could possibly be our last move? What would we do with all the stuff we had accumulated over the years? We liked The Outer Banks! While medical care was quite good for routine medical issues, in the event of serious medical issues likely for the elderly, travel to Duke University in North Carolina or to Norfolk, VA, would be required. Maintenance-free patio homes in The Outer Banks were very limited. The focus in The Outer Banks is on tourism and flood protection.

This started our process of deciding what we wanted in our future residence. We considered the following attributes to be essential: relatively close to as much family as possible, one-floor living, maintenance-free building with yard and shrubbery covered, near major medical center, near major airport, near relatively large city, temperate climate with four seasons. Based on these criteria, we did our research and started looking. Among the places we explored were Little Washington, NC, Greenville, NC, and a retirement community called Atlantic Shores in Virginia Beach, VA. We also looked very seriously in Chesapeake, VA, where I had lived for several years when I was getting started in a new career. This met the criteria of good medical care, closer to family, still some friends in the area, and a great location.

At the same time, we were planning a trip to Rocky Mount, VA, to visit my sisters and to check out commercial property I own in the town. Out of the blue, a light went on in my head. Why don't we check out residential properties in this area? While growing up on a farm in the area I had little chance to experience the major city that was nearby – Roanoke, VA. Roanoke, the Star City of the South, is one of those locations that is a hidden treasure for those who have not experienced it. Conveniently located in the New River Valley and surrounded by the Blue Ridge Mountains, the famous Blue Ridge Parkway traverses the area.

Roanoke is called "The Star City of the South" because of building the world's tallest free-standing star in 1949. The star is located on Mill Mountain and overlooks downtown Roanoke. The electrical star is visible for 60 miles and is a major attraction for locals as well as area tourists.

The beautiful city, surrounded by mountains, is the largest city and metro area in Southwest Virginia. Once the center of railroad activities in the region, Roanoke is now made up of medical, research, and diversified technical industries. Much of Roanoke's research and technical enterprise is in conjunction with Virginia Tech, my alma mater, a large university of over 35,000 students, which is just a short 40-minute drive down the road in Blacksburg, VA. In fact, the airport is named the Roanoke-Blacksburg Regional Airport. While for many years Roanoke was a sleepy little railroad town made up of people who were born there, lived there, and died there, its current industrial base and employment opportunities attract people from all over the country. Additionally, many people traveling on north to south vacations have been captivated by Roanoke's beauty and tranquility and have decided to make it their retirement destination. These same attractive attributes appealed to Mary and me as well.

Life in The Star City

On our first trip to Roanoke from The Outer Banks of North Carolina, we had arranged for a real estate agent to show us some properties. The first few places we visited did not excite us. Toward the end of the day, however, we realized that we were entering a community called Orchard Villas. Our first impression was of the imposing and attractive guardhouse at the entryway. As we drove in, we were overcome with the beauty of the homes constructed of stone and Hardie Plank, the well-manicured lawns and landscaping, the cherry tree-lined streets, and the attractive clubhouse and pool area.

We spotted a man on the street who happened to be Facilities Chairman for the community. We spoke with him briefly, which led to him taking us to one of the homes that he knew would soon go on the market. The family who was in the process of preparing the condo for sale graciously invited us in to show us around. The Facilities Chairman also made us aware that two other homes would soon be going on the market, which enabled us to get in contact with those owners to arrange tours of their condos. We ended up choosing the one owned by a young physician couple who decided to move close to the Carilion Medical Center and VA

Tech Medical School where they worked. The condo featured a sunroom with a view of the road and people passing by, as well as of nearby mountains. The open floor concept, high vaulted ceilings, spacious kitchen with attractive granite countertops and plentiful cabinets, complete with a fireplace, an office, a guest bedroom, and a large master bedroom sealed the deal. Mary and I simultaneously recognized that we had found the community we wanted to live in. Within a few months we were able to make the move.

In the meantime, we started getting rid of excess furniture, tools, small appliances, etc., that we had in our Outer Banks home. In the end, much of the excess was sold at auction in Norfolk, VA. We had no difficulty selling our house in Southern Shores, as it was a desirable house in a premium location. For added value, it was located on a hill with a commanding view of the water-surrounded, treed property.

When the Roanoke property became available, we were ready to move. We did have the luxury of having the new property painted on the inside while it was vacant. As we were getting settled into our new home and community, we quickly discovered it was friendly and neighborly. In fact, two resident ladies with whom we were put in contact, Brenda Lucas and Cheryl Clifton, offered to do some initial cleaning for us since the housecleaner we had hired for a pre-move cleaning had to cancel at the last minute. While the young physician couple who had previously occupied the house were great in many ways, housekeeping was not among their strong points. A deep cleaning was a necessity. To our benefit, our friendly neighbors had already started the process before we arrived. As could be expected, the packing, unpacking, and the move itself presented their challenges, but we both felt it was worth it. Even though we had disposed of much of our furnishings from the NC home, designing a plan to move the remainder of furnishings from a 4000-square-foot-home to an 1800-square-foot-home presented unique challenges.

After we were relatively settled in, we began exploring our immediate community as well as the larger Roanoke metro area. Included in our exploration was a 30-mile trip to the Callaway/Rocky Mount area, the place of my birth and raising where my two sisters were still living. My younger sister, Linda Barnhart, was experiencing early stages of terminal cancer. She later passed away. My older sister, Joyce Ann Jamison, was experiencing her own set of health issues. Her daughter, Jennifer, and Jennifer's husband, Jeff, had recently moved into her home to take care of her. In a strange turn of events, a young and healthy Jennifer was diagnosed with Lou Gehrig's disease, and after a rapid progression of the disease, she passed away. This unforeseen change of events resulted in Joyce Ann moving to Richmond, VA, to be in the care of her granddaughter, Lynanne Jamison.

So, in a matter of two short years, I was the only Sowder sibling living in the area.

We have, however, continued to make Rocky Mount one of the regular places to visit. It gives me the opportunity to check on commercial property that I've owned in downtown Rocky Mount. The property had been in my deceased wife's family for many years, known as the Martin Jewelry store building. The building is currently occupied by the State Farm Insurance Co. and a local beauty shop.

We've also appreciated being closer to VA Tech in Blacksburg, where I have been on the Corps of Cadets Alumni Board of Directors. In that capacity, Mary and I have had the luxury of watching the Hokie's football game in the President's Box. We've enjoyed many other special events at VA Tech as members of the Ut Prosim Society (special donors to VA Tech). One of the special honors of my life was being selected as Distinguished Alumnus of the VA Tech Corps of Cadets for the year 2020.

We enjoy visiting mountain towns and driving the Blue Ridge Parkway. Especially noteworthy have been visits to the Homestead and Greenbrier Resorts located in the southwestern Virginia and West Virginia mountains. Also special to us was a week-long road trip along the famous "Crooked Road". This road highlights the heritage of country and bluegrass music. Along the way are such venues as the famous Galax Fiddlers' Convention; the Floyd Country Store, which attracts bluegrass artists from several surrounding states; the Museum of Country Music in Bristol, VA; the Carter Family homesite; and the outdoor drama in Big Stone Gap, VA – The Trail of the Lonesome Pine. One of the highlights of my ventures in bluegrass music was the opportunity I had to play upright bass with the Floyd Country Store house band.

In our neighborhood, we have much to enjoy. While we checked out several churches, we quickly concluded that Bonsack Baptist Church would be our church home. It is a very large church with six pastors having different responsibilities for worship, administration, seniors, youth, etc. The Senior Pastor, Chris Cadenhead, whom we really appreciate, was educated at Duke University's Methodist Seminary. Most attractive to both Mary and me is arguably the best music program in the Roanoke region. The choir has performed in numerous distinguished venues, including Carnegie Hall in New York City. Both Mary and I have sung in the large choir and have made one tour with the choir to perform at the National Cathedral in Washington, D.C. Also, the church has given me some opportunities to participate in bluegrass music. Mary has been called on to use her musical talent as a substitute organist/pianist at Bonsack Baptist Church and to substitute at other churches in the area.

We have developed many friendships at Bonsack Baptist with so many activities available. One of our favorite social activities is the Wednesday night dinners. At one of our early dinners, Mary stopped by the drink station to pick up her drink. Options were numerous, including both sweetened and unsweetened iced tea. Mary asked the drink attendant, Mike Bryant, our Sunday School teacher, for half sweetened and half unsweetened iced tea. His immediate reply was "Ma'am, in the Baptist church, we do not serve mixed drinks!" Ha! - our first introduction to a fun-loving and very knowledgeable Bible scholar.

When we moved to the Roanoke area, I thought I had finally settled into a life of leisure out of the spotlight. This was not to be! It was discovered that I had previously been a member of the Chesterfield County Board of Supervisors. Chesterfield County has been and still is a model for other municipal governments in Virginia to follow. This is based on Chesterfield's size of 350,000+ residents, the third largest county in Virginia, as well as its efficiency in governing. At the first vacancy, I was singled out and appointed to the Roanoke County Economic Development Authority. While it is early in my tenure, I have already determined that based on our limited undeveloped land, our primary function will be redevelopment. I have also been voted in as a Director of the Military Officers Association of America (MOAA) local chapter. In addition, I volunteer one afternoon a week at the Roanoke/Blacksburg Regional Airport as an Ambassador. We assist newly arriving passengers by answering their questions about local transportation, directions, and general information about the area.

As if all the above was not enough to keep an 86-year-old retiree (from several different occupations) busy; the unexpected, unsolicited, unanticipated, and unwanted became a reality. I let down my serious resistance, my determination to continue saying no, and my desire to have an easy-going, restful, and uncomplicated life. To my dismay, I was elected to the Board of Directors of our 108-home condominium homeowners' association. Moreover, if that was not enough, I was selected President of the Board. Whoop-dee-doo!! To say I am busy is an understatement! As a condominium association, we have many maintenance issues dealing with the exterior of individual buildings and landscaping, issues with contract negotiations, as well as issues with the use of the clubhouse and pool. Fortunately, our neighborhood buildings are relatively new with high quality construction materials, and the community has been expertly managed by my predecessors and our management company. It is a comforting fact for me that our capital reserve is very well funded for the coming years. The time-consuming elements of my job are essentially non-issues in the big picture; issues such as the allowable size of dogs, dog-walking guidelines, allowable plantings, placement of pots and other items on patios, etc. When it's all said and done, most issues are not too serious and in fact often are humorous. We are a community of aging corporate retirees who have been used to living in large homes with essentially unrestricted privileges. Down-sizing and living in a more restrictive environment takes its toll on some individuals. Overall, we love living in the community and the freedom of having the outside maintenance and lawncare taken care of by the association. Most importantly, we have developed great friendships with many residents.

My Bluegrass Music Adventures

I have always had an appreciation of music – many types. From my earliest recollections I sang in church and later in the high school choir. While in the high school choir, I was introduced to the double bass fiddle, also referred to as upright bass. The choir director, Jim Burrell, taught me the essentials of playing the bass in jazz and dance music styles, which led me to become a member of his jazz trio. Jim played piano, Wayne Bennett played saxophone, and I played upright bass. ("If you think you can, you can.") We played a few local gigs as I recall and one out-of-town gig in the mountains of far Southwest Virginia at a place called Craig Healing Springs.

After high school, my music participation took a hiatus for most of my active working life except for attending a few bluegrass festivals. I learned to love bluegrass music. As my work life slowed down after retirement in Richmond, VA, I decided to become involved as a participant in bluegrass music. My first effort was to buy a brand-new Martin guitar. Martins are not cheap; in fact, the most expensive of guitars, the Martin HD28 is the standard for professional bluegrass pickers. If I was going to become involved, I wanted the best that money could buy. Any good Martin guitar will sell for thousands of dollars.

I taught myself to play bluegrass guitar with home study courses, listening to CD's, and just plain trial and error practice. I never became a great guitar picker, but I developed into a reasonably good rhythm guitarist by attending jam sessions in a local church in Richmond, VA. At these jam sessions, professional and well-experienced players showed up, as well as many 'wannabes' like me. Anyone was welcomed to join a group and play along. The professional players were very kind to let others join them in the jam sessions. It was through observing and playing along in these groups that I became a guitar picker and was able to play along and hold my own in a group. ("If you think you can, you can.") I participated in these sessions for several years.

I enjoyed the jam sessions very much but noticed that most of the groups had from two or three up to several guitarists participating. Rarely were upright bass players available. That prompted me to change directions and become a bass player. I ordered an upright bass from

California and could hardly wait for it to arrive. When it did arrive, I started the long road of self-teaching on the bass. After over 40 years, I had forgotten the basics I had learned in high school. Furthermore, playing bass fiddle in bluegrass style is totally different from playing in classical or jazz styles.

So again, I went about learning the basics of playing bass fiddle by first picking on the corresponding guitar strings. The G, D, A, and low E strings on a guitar are the same as the strings on a bass. So, I literally learned the back and forth bass picking technique on the guitar. I was 100% self-taught, as I knew no bass players in the area to ask for assistance. Eventually, I perfected my bass technique by playing along with bluegrass CD's. ("If you think you can, you can!")

Along the way, a couple of friends I went to church with were talking about starting a bluegrass band. Eventually the band was formed and was named Sleepy Hollow Bluegrass Band. The band was complete with banjo, guitar, mandolin, and me on upright bass, as well as two phenomenal female singers. I played in the band for several years until relocating to The Outer Banks of North Carolina. The Sleepy Hollow Bluegrass Band developed a good reputation in the area and was contracted to play many gigs, averaging one or two per month. We also played in regional bluegrass festivals. During the time I was involved with Sleepy Hollow, we recorded a CD with me featured as a soloist on "Blue

Virginia Blues." The band is still going strong today with four of its original members.

Upon moving to The Outer Banks, bluegrass was still in my blood. The Outer Banks hosts one of the largest and most prominent bluegrass festivals in the country. This festival is held in the town of Manteo overlooking the Pamlico Sound. Many nationally known artists view this setting as the best in the country. After getting established in the area, I decided to form my own bluegrass band. I first started with trying to find a fiddle player. I asked Sue Waters, a well-known classical violinist if she thought she could do bluegrass. Sue said, "I grew up with bluegrass and love it," so she consented to be my fiddler. Needing an outstanding vocalist and guitar player, I contacted Amy Denson, our Youth Pastor at Duck United Methodist Church. She qualified on both counts and agreed to join. A music teacher in the Dare County School system, Felicia Byrum, became my mandolin player. Banjo was a challenge! I had two part-timers who played with us on and off, but for most of our performances, it was the three girls and me on bass. I came up with what I thought was a super innovative name for the group – Seagrass. We played for local events up and down The Outer Banks. Most noteworthy, we were featured at the Manteo First-Friday Festival event.

My only claim to fame is that during this period, I played bluegrass at sea. Mary and I booked a cruise in the

Caribbean which was advertised as a bluegrass cruise. Several nationally known bands were on this cruise with one of the bands performing as the main headliner for each day. The MC for this event was Tim White, the MC of the nationally televised program, Song of the Mountains. Tim also had his own band aboard. Each night after the afternoon headline performance, some of the band members got together for a fun jam session. I was fortunate enough, thanks to Mary laying the groundwork, to fill in for Tim White's bass player in one of these jam sessions. I will always treasure this experience.

Since relocating to the Roanoke, VA, area, my bluegrass playing has been more limited. I have had the opportunity to play bass with the Floyd Country Store house band. The Floyd Country Store is a famous old bluegrass venue in the Southwest Virginia area that draws performers and enthusiasts from several states around.

I was also asked to be a part of a bluegrass band that performed for the Easter Sunrise service at our Bonsack Baptist Church here in Roanoke. I do not identify Easter hymns with bluegrass, but nevertheless we did it. It was extremely cold that day, making it very difficult to keep our instruments in tune, not to mention the difficulty in playing, but... "If you think you can, you can!" Also, later I was asked to play with other bluegrass musicians for a large audience at Bonsack Baptist church. This event was truly a bluegrass occasion. We had a great time performing a variety of traditional bluegrass, gospel bluegrass, contemporary bluegrass, and country songs. I very much enjoyed playing with the amazing bluegrass professionals that were in the band. Several months after the performance, I still got compliments and comments from attendees about how much they enjoyed the event.

I still look for opportunities to play, but much more infrequently. Bluegrass has been and still is a passion and hobby for me.

Don playing and singing bass

Don's Seagrass Band, Outer Banks, NC
photo credit Jason Denson

EPILOGUE

My life has been an exciting journey from the simple life of a poor, country farm boy to the privilege of being a part of much of what the nation and world have to offer. During this journey, I have experienced highs and lows, setbacks, and fast forwards. Through it all, I have learned that faith in God as my Father and partner, faith in myself, and faith in and trust of the people I work with are essential to success.

The people I have worked with that have had a positive impact on my journey are far too many to name in this book. If you are one of those individuals and your name did not appear in this writing, "Thank you!!". There is no way I could ever have imagined as a boy that my life would be so exciting, full of adventure, and would lead to involvement in national and worldwide activities.

Mary and I both, due to the grace of God, are in good health. Our plan is to keep on trucking. "If you think you can, you can!!"

In the end, it's all about family. We are blessed to have our children and grandchildren.

<u>Don's children:</u>

Son: Reid Sowder, Richmond, VA, General Manager, Byrd Orthodontics; Owner, Commonwealth Timing and Race Management; married to Cheryl, homemaker

Daughter: Allison White, Richmond, VA, Pharmacist; married to Dr. Paul White, White Orthodontics

Son: Stuart Sowder, New York City, V.P. Pfizer Pharmaceuticals; partner, Rusty Yuson, Yuson & Irvine Law Firm

<u>Mary's children:</u>

Daughter: Andrea Slaton, Tyler, Texas, homemaker, Childcare Coordinator; married to Marvin Slaton, Co-founder and Executive Director, Modern Day – Christian missionary organization

Daughter: Heather Nutt, Mineola, Texas, Teacher; married to John Nutt, Paladin Solutions Security, and his own woodworking business

Grandchildren:

Reid – John, Donna, Ellen

Allison – Trey, Tanner

Stuart – Lucas, Lyla

Andrea – Judah, Isaiah, Lydiah

Heather – Lilah, Colton

Great-grandchildren:

John – Naomi, Reid

People Significantly Impacting My Life:

Dick and Virginia Sowder – my parents

Bernice Jamison – my childhood Sunday School teacher

Berman Flora – a regional 4-H Club advisor

Brud and Mary Sowder – my grandparents

Beverly Reid Sowder – my high school sweetheart and deceased wife

Bruce and Sue Reid – Beverly's parents

Eleanor and Charles Easter – Beverly's sister and her husband

Carl Bussey – Zone Manager, Sealtest Foods – my uncle and mentor

George Henley – Air Force ROTC instructor; neighbor

Ann and Les Miller – early neighbors and long-term friends in Norfolk, VA (and in The Outer Banks, NC)

Jim Anderson – Upjohn rep and friend

General Tommy Thompson – Regimental Commander, VA Tech Corps of Cadets, Fellow Battery Commander, 111th Field Artillery

LTC Harry Kocen, Battalion Commander, Virginia National Guard

Joe Young – my District Manager, Lederle Labs

Jim Wallin – my Regional Manager, Lederle Labs

John Rose – Director Training and Educational Services, Lederle Labs, Pearl River, NY, my boss

Jim Skinner – Director of Sales, Lederle Laboratories, Wayne, NJ, my boss

John Walker – Manager Government Sales, Lederle Labs, Washington, DC, my predecessor

Fred Daussin – my boss - later employee, Lederle Labs

Brigadier General Al Bryant – Director, Dept. of Veterans Affairs Pharmacy Services and friend

O.T. Jamison – cousin, neighbor, and friend, Fairfax, VA

Col. Jack Robinson – Commander 2070th USAR School

Larry Tilton – VP of Sales, Lederle Laboratories, Wayne, NJ; my boss; later, President of Lederle Laboratories

Bob Saydah – VP of Sales, Lederle Laboratories, Wayne, NJ, my boss

Dave (and Sylvia) Bethune – started with me as a Lederle representative, became President of Lederle and Executive VP of American Cyanamid Co., special friend for over 60 years

Al and Billy Stubmann – very special friends in Franklin Lakes, NJ

Dick and Roseanne Parr - neighbors and friends in Wyckoff, NJ

Jim and Betty Bacon – Regional Director, Lederle Labs, Denver, CO, long-term special friends

General Willard Scott – Superintendent, U.S. Military Academy West Point, my boss

Colonel Pierce Rushton – Director of Admission, U.S. Military Academy West Point, my boss

Colonel Ross Crossley – Commander 5th Division Artillery, my boss

John Goodwin – VP Sales, Lederle Labs, my boss

Marie Quinn – Republican activist, my campaign advisor, Chesterfield, VA

Dickie King – fellow member, Board of Supervisors, Chesterfield County, VA

Sander Flaum – CEO, Robert A Becker, Inc., New York City, business partner

Rev. Al Schrader – retired Methodist minister, good friend and golf partner

Jim Gilmore – Former VA Governor and campaign supporter and friend

George Allen – Former VA Governor, US Senator, special friend and campaign supporter

John Watkins - VA State Senator, campaign supporter and friend

Colonel T.O. Williams – VA Tech classmate and long-term special friend

David Purdy – President, Psychological Consultants, friend and employer

Barbara Grimes – tenant in living quarters of our Dominion Valley Drive home and special friend

Calvin and Eula Lucy – special friends and campaign supporters

Members of Sleepy Hollow and Seagrass Bluegrass Bands

Robert Hodges – friend and campaign supporter

Gene James – CEO Southern States, Inc.; Chairman of Board, Virginia United Methodist Homes; friend

Major General Jerry Allen - Commandant, VA Tech Corps of Cadets

Mary Hudson Sowder - my second wife, best friend and supporter

Jimmy Benson – real estate advisor and friend

John Grady Sowder – District Judge, uncle, and good friend

Bill and Dyan Crone – neighbors and friends in Corolla, NC, co-worker Corolla Wild Horse Fund

Dr. George Grinnan – fellow choir member at Duck UMC and friend

Colonel Gary (Chap) Moore and Taunya – special friends in The Outer Banks, NC

Tom and Jayne Bennett – former Mayor of Southern Shores, NC, friends

Diana Johnson – special friend in Kitty Hawk, NC

Reese Evans – General Contractor, cousin and friend, Outer Banks, NC

Michael and Nancy Terry – special friends in The Outer Banks, NC, and Charlottesville, VA

Lt. General Paul Myers, Surgeon General, US Air Force

Lt. General Frank Ledford, Surgeon General, U.S. Army

Significant (Memorable) Life Events

- born at home (1937) in a house with no electricity or indoor plumbing
- rode a Greyhound bus from Rocky Mount, VA, to Jacksonville, FL, as a child with my older (12-year-old) sister
- received my own calf from state 4-H Club to raise and then to give its first offspring to another 4-H Club member
- permitted for the first time to drive a car to Roanoke, VA, alone
- met Beverly, my first wife, at Franklin County High School
- elected to be President, Student Body, Franklin County High School
- selected to be the VA National Guard Battalion Commander's driver for a town parade
- first active-duty training with VA National Guard at Bethany Beach, Delaware
- first day of college at VA Tech
- selected for membership in the German Club – VA Tech
- bought my first car, a 1954 Plymouth
- married my first wife, Beverly
- graduated from VA Tech; commissioned a 2nd Lieutenant, U.S. Army
- first Army assignment, Fort Sill, OK
- births of all three children – Reid, Allison, Stuart

- first civilian job — territory salesman, Sealtest Foods, Norfolk, VA
- purchased first home, Goldcrest Drive, Chesapeake, VA
- changed careers — to pharmaceutical sales representative, Lederle Laboratories, Norfolk, VA
- won Lederle's Gold Cup award four years in a row for outstanding sales achievement, a company record at the time
- won American Cyanamid Company's Golden Oval award for outstanding sales achievement in all divisions
- promoted to Battery Commander, Virginia National Guard
- promoted to District Manager, Lederle Laboratories, Washington DC
- promoted to National Sales Training Manager, Pearl River, NY
- promoted to Manager, Federal Government Affairs, Washington DC
- development and assisting in promotion of my government account managers, i.e. David Shadeed to Chicago District Manager to South Atlantic Regional Director
- elected to be Chairman, Sustaining Members, Association of Military Surgeons of the United States

- met Vice-President George H. W. Bush at a small private birthday party for Congressman Sonny Montgomery
- promoted to National Hospital and Government Sales Manager, Lederle Laboratories, Wayne, NJ
- established and served as first Director of National Oncology Sales
- promoted to Lt. Colonel, U.S. Army Reserve
- taught Army Reserve officers (who were airline pilots) in the U.S. Army Command and General Staff College at West Chester Airport, NY
- after retiring from Lederle Laboratories, purchased a 5-acre estate with tennis courts in a premium neighborhood of Fairfax, VA
- conducted medical seminars for Boron-Lepore throughout the U.S.
- set up a business in New York City for Robert A. Becker Company – Peer Perspectives
- vacationed during 4th of July weeks with family at our Corolla, NC, beach house
- set up a meeting for Dave Bethune with the Chairman of the Senate Veterans Affairs Committee
- visited my son, Reid, during his stay at Loma Linda, CA, Hospital due to a life-threatening brain hemorrhage
- moved to Richmond, VA – a second post-retirement move

- assessed personnel from various pharmaceutical companies for Psychological Consultants, Inc. – became Vice-President, Sales and Marketing
- promoted to Colonel, U.S. Army – served as West Point Inspector General IMA as well as a Field Admissions Officer
- became very active in the Chesterfield County Republican Party
- ran for and was elected to the Chesterfield County Board of Supervisors
- served for several years on the Board and became Chairman of the Board, Virginia United Methodist Homes, Inc.
- lost the love of my life, Beverly, to pancreatic cancer
- was very active at River Road United Methodist Church – choir, committees, etc. – met my second wife, Mary, who was the Music Director/Organist
- as a high-end car 'buff', purchased several over the years: Lincoln, Jaguar, Cadillac, BMW, etc.
- delighted in my children's marriages, as well as the births and growing-up years of all grandchildren
- after living the lonesome life of a bachelor for a while, married my second wife, Mary, a Godsend
- purchased several rental properties in the Richmond, VA, area over a few years

- moved to my Corolla, NC, property with my wife, Mary
- enjoyed living in The Outer Banks of North Carolina for about 9 years
- worked with the Corolla Wild Horse Fund for several years (one of my favorite jobs) - took people up the beach and over the dunes on tours in search of wild horses
- experienced the effect of moderate hurricanes while living in The Outer Banks
- elected to be Commodore Southern Shores Boat Club
- appointed to the Southern Shores, NC, Planning Board
- used my experience with The Sleepy Hollow Bluegrass Band in Richmond, VA, to form my own band in The Outer Banks, which I named "Seagrass"
- completed prostate cancer treatment – 2 years of radiation and hormone therapy
- elected President, Orchard Villas Homeowners' Association
- appointed to Roanoke County Economic Development Authority

Made in the USA
Columbia, SC
02 May 2024

35187789R00093